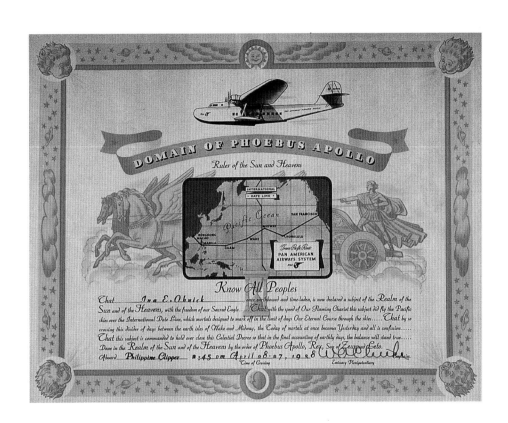

DOMAIN OF PHOEBUS APOLLO

Ruler of the Sun and Heavens

Know All Peoples

That *Ira E. Ohnick*, once earthbound and time-laden, is now declared a subject of the Realm of the Sun and of the Heavens, with the freedom of our Sacred Eagle..... That with the speed of Our Flaming Chariot this subject did fly the Pacific skies over the International Date Line, which mortals designed to mark off in the limit of days Our Eternal Course through the skies..... That by so crossing this divider of days between the earth isles of Wake and Midway, the Today of mortals at once becomes Yesterday and all is confusion..... That this subject is commanded to hold ever close this Celestial Decree so that in the final accounting of earthly days, the balance will stand true..... Done in the Realm of the Sun and of the Heavens by the order of Phoebus Apollo, Rex, Son of Zeus and Leto.

Aboard **Philippine Clipper** **2:45 pm April 26-27, 1938**

Time of Crossing   Emissary Plenipotentiary   Captain

CLASSIC
AMERICAN AIRLINES

Geza Szurovy

Photography by Martin Berinstein

ZENITH
PRESS

Dedication
For Anne

Front cover: Albuquerque's adobe-revival terminal was one of the first attempts at giving airport architecture a local dimension and some flair beyond bland functionality. It still exists, although the airport it served has been long turned over to developers in favor of a new, larger airport.

Frontis: An international dateline crossing certificate issued to Ina E. Ohnick on April 28, 1938. Prodigious travelers to the Far East, such as the Ohnick family, accumulated many such certificates before World War II put Pacific travel on hold. On today's transpacific flights, we just reset our watches.

Title page: The DC-3 is the longest continuously serving airliner in the world. Almost seven decades after its first flight there are still well over 100 DC-3s in regular service. *Lawrence Feir*

Back cover, top: This American Airlines Convair 880 performs an impressive takeoff on a very long runway. The takeoff is somewhat staged for the cameras, as the early jets had rather anemic takeoff performance when fully loaded with fuel and passengers for a transcontinental flight.

Printed in Hong Kong

contents

Acknowledgments

It is daunting to face the challenge of distilling a subject as vast as the history of America's airlines into a framework that fits within the editorial constraints of a single book. Fortunately the task is made easier by the efforts of those who dedicate themselves to looking after our aviation heritage in the nation's museums, archives, historical societies, restoration groups, and private memorabilia collections. Without their knowledge of the field, the professional preservation of documents, photographs, artifacts, and entire airplanes (and their willingness to help), it would have been impossible to produce Classic American Airlines.

I am particularly indebted to the Seattle Museum of Flight for giving photographer Martin Berinstein and me unreserved access to its airline materials. Thanks to curator, Dennis Parks, who was most generous with his support, and Katherine Williams, whose impressive knowledge of the collection, energetic assistance, and enthusiasm for the subject were key contributions, and Christine Runte, the collection's registrar. Due to space constraints, no major museum can come close to exhibiting its entire wealth of material, so it gives me great pleasure to be able to thank the Museum of Flight for its hospitality by showcasing some of the rarely seen items from its airline collection.

Indispensable archival support came from Boeing; one of few aviation companies that continues to provide easy access to its photographic archives for authors and researchers. Since its acquisition of McDonnell Douglas, Boeing also owns the Douglas archives, which assures continued access to this valuable source and simplifies a researcher's life. Thanks to Boeing's Mike Lombardi in Seattle, Pat McGinnis in Long Beach, and Karin Jones in Permissions Licensing, whose cheerful efficiency provided a timely response to any request.

Acknowledgment is also due to the community of airline memorabilia collectors, whose periodic trade shows yielded some of the best artifacts and photos featured; and to the aviation writers whose reference books provided valuable source material. R. E. G. Davies' *Airlines of the United States Since 1914* is an especially outstanding reference work (and is thankfully back in print). The books of Robert Serling, one of America's most prolific aviation historians, also deserve special mention, as does the Journal of the American Aviation Historical Society, which features important historical monographs on airlines and airliners. The airline veterans, interviewed for this book and over the years on related topics, also made a crucial contribution.

I would like to thank my friend, Martin Berinstein, for his superb memorabilia photography specifically for this book, the substantial additional photo support, and letting me hide in his Boston studio to finish the project; to photographer Lawrence Feir for sharing his growing collection of stunning vintage airliner portraits; and to my friend and editor, Mike Haenggi, whose support was instant and unequivocal, and who bore my badgering over deadlines and the inclusion of extra photos with his usual patience and good humor.

Introduction

To some people, getting on an airliner today is about as exciting as boarding a bus. One leading airline manufacturer, coming late to the game, recognized this when it named its venture Airbus. But this was not always so. There was a time when boarding an airliner was charged with the possibility of physical danger, adventure, glamour, and a sense of swift reach that we can no longer appreciate. Advances in safety rapidly lessened the risks of going by air to levels comparable with journeys by other means, but the excitement remained for decades until the technology of flight matured to the point of turning flying into just another form of mass transit.

Classic American Airlines looks back on those earlier, more stimulating days when aviation was the equivalent of today's high tech industry. It was a time when progress was so rapid that the latest airliners were obsolete even as they started rolling off the assembly line, airline stocks could go up tenfold in a matter of weeks and collapse with equal alacrity, and the price of an engineering or pilot error was measured in lost lives and aircraft. In contrast to todays software entrepreneurs, test pilots like Boeing's Eddie Allen couldn't just hit Ctrl-Alt-Del if something went wrong.

The story starts in the mid-1920s when America's first airlines were formed. It traces the emergence of the airlines that endured and recounts the development of the important airliners and the nation's air transport system. It ends in the early 1970s with the advent of the widebody era and the energy crisis that quadrupled aviation fuel prices and started the two decades of unprecedented industry turbulence intensified by deregulation that forever changed the world of America's airlines.

Chapter One briefly reviews the infrastructural progress and major technological developments during the period covered. The following chapters each cover one of the eleven airlines that mattered the most and lasted the course. Other airlines that played important roles but were acquired by competitors are also covered.

A separate chapter on each airline runs the risk of some redundancy. This was minimized by addressing a particular aircraft type, or new development in detail, only in connection with the airlines that took the lead in introducing them. Thus, the Constellation's development is covered in the chapter on Trans World Airlines, while the 747 story is addressed in the chapter on Pan American.

The advantage of airline specific chapters is the opportunity to give them all their due, including the smaller ones that tend to get suppressed in all-encompassing chronological histories. It is worthwhile for all readers to first read Chapter One, which sets the stage, but beyond that everyone should feel free to proceed to any airline of preference to look back through its window into the past.

Air Transport Age

In 500 years the twentieth century will be remembered as the Age of Mobility, and its enduring symbol will be the airliner. Historians will marvel at how our society progressed in only 66 years from the Wright Flyer to the Boeing 747. They will most likely conclude that the leader in commercial aviation during those years was America's aviation industry and its airlines, not because Americans were more talented or inventive than others, but because they were better able to commercialize innovation. Indeed, much of the early technical innovation that made such wondrous progress possible came from across the Atlantic.

In the first 25 years after the Wright's groundbreaking hop, European governments and businesses embraced aviation far more enthusiastically than their American counterparts. In 1922, when most Americans would have thought that Marconi was a pasta, British pilots were routinely taking cross bearings on Marconi radio beacons to find their destinations. Concurrently, Germany's Professor Junkers built the first all-metal, cantilever winged airliner, the F-13, made of an exciting, new lightweight alloy called duraluminum that was strong, yet pliable and corrosion resistant. And British and French airlines were running five-course champagne lunch flights between Paris and London.

The first airliners that would dominate America's first serious foray into air transportation were designed and built by a Dutchman, Anthony Fokker. In coming decades, the principles of advanced aerodynamics were established in large measure by German research organizations, and the commercial jet age became Britain's to throw away.

So how was it that America's role became preeminent? Of the many reasons, two stand out in particular. Primarily, during this period the United States proved to be the most adept at what Americans affectionately call their ability to get the job done. No other society could come close to having the required level of organizational skill to take promising innovations, raise the requisite capital, and turn them into booming large-scale commercial enterprises. Secondly, Europe's ability to play a bigger role was devastated by World War II. Economically all of Europe lost the war, and the postwar economic structure took decades to evolve to the point where the region could once again effectively compete with the United States.

Ironically, in spite of America's vision of itself as a land of free-wheeling Darwinian entrepreneurs, the airline industry was created with massive government support, and competition was tightly regulated until 1978. However, unlike in Europe, where

The golden age of piston liners is brought alive by this Boeing 377 Stratocruiser's 3,500-horsepower Pratt & Whitney engines over hostile terrain. In reality the engine was problematic because it was pushed to the edge of its technological limits. Failures were so frequent that the Stratocruiser was nicknamed the best three-engined airliner over the Atlantic.

All in the family. The Boeing 247, the first modern airliner, is dwarfed by its direct descendant, the Boeing 747. The *William M. Allen*, is a United jet, named after Boeing's long-serving president who oversaw the transition to jets and widebodies.

most national airlines were directly owned by the government and their losses were fully underwritten, the U.S. government provided a subsidy via the air mail and stage-managed competition among private companies. Within this framework, the industry slowly evolved, passing important regulatory and technical milestones along the way.

In the early 1920s, no airplane existed that could make money in passenger service without a subsidy. The day's rudimentary airliners didn't have enough seats to pay operating costs at ticket prices a handful of adventurous passengers were willing to pay. Air mail, however, was becoming increasingly popular, carried by a fleet of surplus World War I DeHavilland DH-4s operated by the U.S. Post Office.

As this operation grew, the post office became increasingly concerned about being ill equipped to run an expanding aviation business. Political pressure sought to turn over the function to the private sector, modeled on its long-standing mail carriage arrangements with the railroads. In 1925 Congress passed the Kelly Contract Air Mail Act, which put up the air mail routes for bids by private companies. It was closely followed by the 1926 Air Commerce Act, which for the first time set out laws governing aircraft operations and required pilots to earn licenses. These two pieces of legislation were the foundations of modern commercial aviation in the United States.

In this initial phase, air mail was paid for by the pound carried, which provided highly unpredictable cash flows and led some enterprising operators to send themselves massive amounts of mail and slip bricks into the mail sacks. Romantic adventurers flocked to establish scores of grassroots flying services hoping to haul the mail. Many were also eager to carry passengers, which they were allowed to do under the legislation, and turned to Anthony Fokker's airliners and a variety of locally created derivatives.

Following the passage of the Kelly Act, contract air mail flying didn't get underway in earnest until about 1927, when Charles Lindbergh's solo flight from New York to Paris drove the United States plane crazy overnight. Aviation turned into the high-tech industry of the day, and big business became convinced of the money to be made. Millions of dollars poured into rapidly formed conglomerates that created airplane manufacturers; engine, propeller, and aircraft systems makers; and airlines supported by the mail subsidies to use their sister companies' products.

But it proved tough to make money in airline flying even with the subsidies. Predicting in advance the volume of mail on a route was difficult, and the pressure to place a low bid to get the business eroded

The St. Petersburg–Tampa Airboat Line is generally recognized as the first airline. Founded in 1914, it charged its first passenger, the Mayor of Tampa, $400 for the 23-minute flight, although the regular fares were more reasonable. Lack of demand led to its early demise.

Aircraft Fleet Size Growth

The increases in fleet size among the airlines covered in this book give a rough indication of their progress relative to each other as well as progress overall. Pan American is shown separately because it flew only on international routes.

The dates are significant. In 1942 the airlines were required to assign half their fleet to Air Transport Command service. The figures are prior to the transfer. In 1958 the jet era began for U.S. airlines with scheduled service of the Boeing 707. And 1969 was the last year before the introduction of the Boeing 747, the first and largest of the widebodies.

In 1942 approximately 90 percent of the airliners were DC-3s. The 1950s were the golden age of the piston liners, and by 1969 the majority of the airliners were jets. While the number of aircraft increased steadily, the number of available seats increased at a more rapid pace as the airliners got bigger. For an idea of passenger growth, see the next sidebar.

Aircraft Fleet Size

	1942	1958	1969
American	74	201	247
United	62	198	386
Eastern	39	187	240
TWA	40	198	232
Northwest	14	55	118
Delta	9	77	129
Continental	6	46	54
Braniff	15	73	76
National	5	52	50
Western	17	32	82
Pan American		151	158

Source: R. E. G. Davies, *Airlines of the United States Since 1914.*

So You're Going to Fly

PASSENGERS on "Trip Three" show their tickets as they board the coast-to-coast liner, right, and their names are checked on the manifest. Above, stewardess and co-pilot examine records at start of the flight from Newark to California.

Passenger brochures went out of their way to reassure travelers about the safety and routine nature of what for them was an alien and often frightening adventure.

profit potential. Most mail carriers flew in the red. However, the increasing size and performance of the aircraft proved air transport had a future, which the airlines would stand a much better chance of reaching with more government help. And by 1930, help was forthcoming through a change in legislation, championed by Postmaster General Walter Folger Brown and a handful of airline lobbyists.

Brown had a visionary commitment to forging the sustainable foundations of a national air transport industry with substantial government assistance. His tool was the 1930 Watres-McNary Act, which changed the air mail subsidy rate from per pound carried to cargo space available for mail carriage regardless of whether mail was actually carried on a particular flight. It also gave sweeping powers to Brown to award air mail routes not to the lowest bidder but to the one who in his judgment was best suited overall to serve the route.

Brown set strict qualifying standards for airlines to be eligible to bid. Mail carriers who had been in business over a 250-mile route for two years could claim pioneering rights and obtain a 10-year certificate to encourage long-term investment. This standard eliminated many small companies from retaining their current routes. In addition, bidders had to have a minimum of six months of night flying experience, further narrowing the field.

Brown then redrew the U.S. air transport map. At a series of meetings with eligible airlines that came to be known as the spoils conferences, he allocated three transcontinental routes and favored one dominant carrier to serve the eastern population centers. His efforts brought into being what came to be known as the Big Four carriers—United, TWA, American, and Eastern—which accounted for 90 percent of airline services nationwide. With such a market share and the redefined method of mail subsidies, the stage was set for these airlines to become viable business entities, capable of realizing the fledgling industry's vast potential. The remainder went to a handful of small, regional carriers, among them Northwest Airlines.

WHY DODGE THIS QUESTION:

Afraid to Fly?

AMERICAN
AIRLINES INC.

This *Life* cover captures the publics fascination with how Pan American's flying boats were perceived to be shrinking the world. In reality the global reach of the handful of Martin 130s and Boeing 314s was more symbolic of the future's potential than commercially substantive.

In 1937 the airline industry was hit by a series of accidents that resulted in a sharp drop in passenger bookings. Breaking an industry taboo on publicly confronting the safety question, C. R. Smith, president of American Airlines responded with this advertisement, which was appreciated by the public for frankly clearing the air.

A TWA Boeing 307 Stratoliner cruising in pressurized comfort high above the weather. While the 307 was too small and slow for a four-engined airliner to be commercially viable, it was an important step forward as the world's first pressurized airliner and deserves more credit than it gets.

Brown and the Republican administration he served were gone by early 1933, casualties of Franklin D. Roosevelt's landslide election victory. Trust-busting Democrats were self-righteously seeking any opportunity to battle "Big Business." Much of their effort was legitimate, but in the case of civil aviation, their zeal threatened the very existence of a fragile industry. The catalyst for chaos was Congressman Hugo Black's investigation of Brown's spoils conferences. Charging bid rigging, Black managed to convince Roosevelt, who had a propensity for shooting from the hip, to abruptly cancel all air mail contracts in February 1934, and hand over the task to a hastily formed Army Air Mail Service, with disastrous results.

The Army fliers were woefully unqualified for their new responsibility because their military flying experience was completely different from what was required to fly the mail on a schedule coast to coast. Within five weeks of assuming responsibility for the mail in the middle of winter, 12 Army pilots were dead. Realizing what he had wrought, a supremely self-confident Roosevelt equally abruptly decreed a return of the mail contracts to the airlines through a new round of bidding.

The result was the 1934 Air Mail Act. It divided responsibility between the post office for assigning the routes, the Interstate Commerce Commission for setting the rates (as it did for railroad and trucking rates), and the Bureau of Commerce for regulating

By the end of the 1930s, dozens of airliners had come into being and many had come and gone. The survivors had no inkling that within two decades they would be flying jets carrying 120 passengers at near the speed of sound. *Martin Berinstein*

The Lockheed Constellation is believed by many to be the most graceful propliner ever built. This Connie, preserved by the Save A Connie Foundation of Kansas City, Missouri, is an 1049H model dressed up as a 1049 Super G, the best of the series. The Constellation's cockpit was cosy and the airplane's complexity contributed to the mandatory creation of the flight engineer's post and labor arguments about the required qualifications. *Lawrence Feir*

operations and safety. As a face-saving fiction, no airline that participated in the spoils conferences could rebid, but a simple change of corporate name satisfied the requirement and within four months, the majority of routes went back to the airlines that originally held them. A handful of newcomers, however, would rise to prominence, such as Delta, Braniff, and National. The act also instructed the aviation conglomerates to divest their airlines from their manufacturing interests.

As the industry took off with the introduction of the Boeing 247 and the Douglas DC-2 and DC-3, another round of far-reaching regulatory refinements was put in place under the Air Mail Act of 1938. Aviation was becoming too specialized and large scale to be handled directly by the Interstate Commerce Commission and the Bureau of Commerce. A separate five person Civil Aviation Authority (CAA) was set up to regulate airline tariffs and air mail rates and

In the golden age of the propliners on prestige runs, such as Transatlantic Boeing Stratocruiser service, the journey was an event and passengers dressed for it. Economy class, however, introduced as Air Coach in 1948 was never nearly as glamorous, and air traffic congestion and ensuing delays and holding patterns were also a problem around major population centers.

assign route certificates. Within the CAA an office of the Administrator was established to oversee and regulate operations, air navigation, and the airways, and an Air Safety Board was created to deal with safety and investigate accidents.

Two years later the Civil Aviation Authority became the Civil Aviation Board (CAB), which went on to control route allocations and ration competition until deregulation in 1978. The CAB's approach over the coming decades was to gradually increase competition within the system by approving an increasing number of competing airlines to serve the same routes as it saw the industry mature.

Traffic Growth

The growth in passenger miles reveals the exponential expansion of airline travel during the 27 years from the beginning of World War II to the dawn of the widebody era. The increase in the available seats and the speed at which those seats could be circulated within the airline system sent passenger volumes soaring. While the era before World War II was the period during which the foundations of the airline industry were laid, the traffic volumes were relatively modest even though the available technology was pushed to its then known limits. The 1950s saw a big increase in available seats as the piston liner's capacity passed 100 passengers, but the most dramatic growth came with the jets not only because of an additional increase in seating capacity but because of the tremendous increase in speed. The combined factors sent capacity soaring and created economies of scale that made air travel widely affordable.

Passenger Miles (millions)

	1942	1958	1969
American	402	5,021	16,296
United	279	5,214	25,485
Eastern	218	4,290	14,002
TWA	202	4,593	19,150
Northwest	52	1,435	7,481
Delta	33	1,467	8,875
Continental	10	423	5,729
Braniff	50	1,008	5,999
National	15	1,070	4,276
Western	28	533	3,721
Pan American	225	3,894	17,058

Source: R. E. G. Davies, *Airlines of the United States Since 1914.*

The DC-7's turbo-compound engines featured powerful turbochargers that added an extra 150 hp per engine to make it the fastest propliner and the first to be able to cross the U.S. continent nonstop in both directions under most wind conditions. The engines were, however, so pushed to their technological limits that failures were endemic and the associated cost made the airplane marginally profitable.

The DC-7 was developed at American Airlines' instigation to compete with TWA's Super Constellation. Pan American was behind its final variant, the DC-7C. The need for the DC-7 was questioned because the jet age was perceived to be around the corner by the time it was launched in 1952, but the airlines got a good eight years out of it in passenger service and many more as a freighter.

The Administrator's office became the Civil Aeronautics Administration, which eventually turned into today's Federal Aviation Administration (FAA), and the Air Safety Board became the aviation arm of the independent National Transportation Safety Board (NTSB).

Within this regulatory framework the airlines grew up, incrementally incorporating a vast array of technological advances. Several milestones are particularly memorable, for they were breakthroughs that pushed the airlines to the next level of progress along the path that ultimately led to the Boeing 747 and its operating environment.

The eternal challenge in aircraft design is conjuring up the lightest, most aerodynamic airframe and mating it with the most powerful engine available in a combination that allows the airplane to carry the desired payload over the required distance economically. Thus dramatic advances develop when a radically new way is found to increase airframe efficiency or engine power. Two developments played decisive roles in making possible the modern airliner that emerged in the mid-1930s: the refinement of lightweight monocoque all-metal airframe construction that incorporated the cantilever wing, and the emergence of light, powerful Pratt & Whitney and Wright air-cooled radial engines.

The key advances in modern airframe design were pioneered by several aircraft manufacturers during the early 1930s, among them Lockheed with

its Orions, the Northrop Alpha, and the Boeing Mailwing. Monocoque fuselage construction, which used the airframe's skin as a load-bearing element, yielded exceptionally light, strong structures. The cantilever wing eliminated the need for struts and flying wires, the greatest agents of drag on early airframes. The Alpha's and Mailwing's duraluminum construction eliminated the danger of wood rot, yet provided as light a structure as the airframes of Lockheed's wooden Orions. All the designs incorporated retractable gear and elaborate fairings. Their designs dramatically reduced drag and yielded a quantum leap in performance.

Pratt & Whitney and Wright created the fundamental piston aero engine that formed the basis for the 3,500-horsepower monsters that propelled the piston fleet toward the end of its golden age. Pratt &

In 1957 the number of passengers crossing the Atlantic by air exceeded for the first time the number of passengers going by ship. The era of mass air travel had truly arrived. A Pan American Boeing Stratocruiser salutes the *Queen Elizabeth* off the coast of Long Island as they both set course for England.

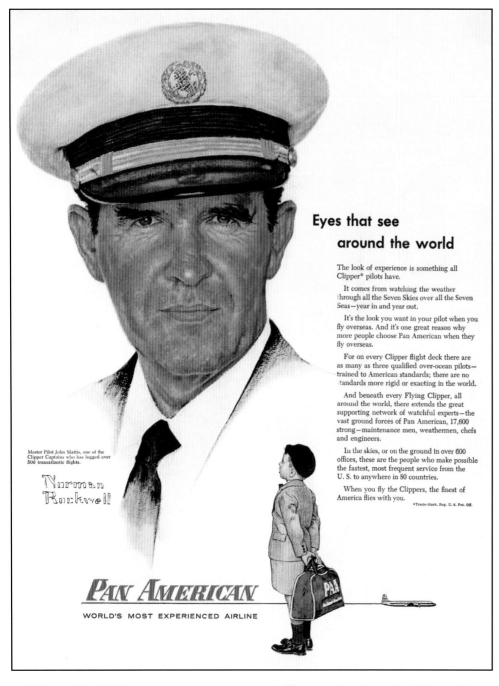

Eyes that see around the world

The look of experience is something all Clipper® pilots have.

It comes from watching the weather through all the Seven Skies over all the Seven Seas—year in and year out.

It's the look you want in your pilot when you fly overseas. And it's one great reason why more people choose Pan American when they fly overseas.

For on every Clipper flight deck there are as many as three qualified over-ocean pilots—trained to American standards; there are no standards more rigid or exacting in the world.

And beneath every Flying Clipper, all around the world, there extends the great supporting network of watchful experts—the vast ground forces of Pan American, 17,600 strong—maintenance men, weathermen, chefs and engineers.

In the skies, or on the ground in over 600 offices, these are the people who make possible the fastest, most frequent service from the U. S. to anywhere in 80 countries.

When you fly the Clippers, the finest of America flies with you.

*Trade-Mark, Reg. U. S. Pat. Off.

Master Pilot John Mattis, one of the Clipper Captains who has logged over 500 transatlantic flights.

Norman Rockwell

PAN AMERICAN

WORLD'S MOST EXPERIENCED AIRLINE

As late as the 1950s, many passengers were still apprehensive about boarding an airliner. This advertisement reassures them by highlighting the overwhelming experience of Pan American's senior captains. It is painted by Norman Rockwell, whose style was heavily imitated by other aviation advertising artists.

Whitneys and Wrights in the 500–700-horsepower range were light and powerful enough to allow the modern airframes to which they were mated to realize their full potential.

The first modern airliner to benefit from these developments was the 10-seat Boeing 247, and at 160 miles per hour it was over 30 percent faster than the lumbering Ford Trimotor. The Douglas DC-2's upstaging of the Boeing 247 is one of the best-known stories in aviation, but Douglas didn't apply any additional new technology to pull off its coup. It merely applied the same technology to greater advantage. The DC-3 did the same to the DC-2 and was the first airplane to find the magic formula to haul enough seats at a cost that enabled it to make a profit without any subsidy.

The DC-3 soon dominated the world, and systems innovations and advances in communication and navigation aids during the 1930s made it a safer and better airplane. Constant speed propellers were a big boost, optimizing climb and cruise performance. The gyroscopic heading indicator, and the artificial horizon developed by Sperry Gyroscope and rather dramatically demonstrated by Jimmy Doolittle in a completely blind landing, opened up the path to safe blind flight. Deicing boots brought under control a big fear of early aviators. Two-way radio communication became standard and radio beacons developed by RCA emitted Morse code to enable airliners for the first time to ride the beam of invisible highways across the sky, as the government assumed the air traffic control system started by American Airlines.

The next important step in aircraft design was the development of the turbo-supercharger that opened up safe high-altitude flight, dramatically boosting engine performance and making possible cabin pressurization to support life above 10,000 feet without the need for oxygen masks. First proposed in Switzerland in 1906 and created by General Electric (GE), it was essentially an air compressor that could fool engines and passenger cabins at altitude into believing that they were in denser, life- and performance-sustaining air. Its small compressor turbine whined at over 30,000 rpm, requiring GE to make advances in metals technology that would stand it in good stead within a few years when it built the first U.S. jet engine.

The first pressurized, supercharged airliner was the Boeing 307 Stratoliner, which deserves more recognition than it gets. It was a derivative of the Boeing B-17 bombers, sharing its wings, empennage, and supercharged engines, but led the commercial application of cabin pressurization. It was also one of

The introduction of jetliners required new airport facilities to handle the increased flow of passengers and their baggage at major airports, but regional fields retained their local character for years to come.

First flight of the Dash 80, Boeing's prototype 707 that commercialized jet travel. Preceded by Britain's DeHavilland Comet, seen here on an early test flight, the 707 prevailed not only because of the setbacks the Comet suffered in a series of tragic crashes caused by a window frame design fault that set off explosive decompression, but because it was bigger and more profitable to operate.

the first airplanes to benefit from the high-octane fuel developed to maximize the performance of the superchargers.

Even though it is widely assumed that World War II played a major role in piston airline development, initially it was the war effort that benefited from the fundamentals of advanced piston technology that were already in place by the time Pearl Harbor was attacked. The DC-4 and the Lockheed Constellation were both in the advanced stages of prototype construction, and the pressurized DC-6 wasn't far behind.

A comparison of aircraft numbers best puts in perspective World War II's technical contribution to U.S. air transportation. On the eve of Pearl Harbor the total U.S. airline fleet consisted of 322 aircraft, 260 of which were DC-3s. In contrast, more than 11,000 C-47s (the DC-3's military version) were built during the war. More than 12,000 Boeing B-17 Flying Fortresses, 18,000 Consolidated B-24 Liberators, and 1,600 military versions of the DC-4 were also built. Such levels of mass production laid the foundations of a postwar aerospace industry on a mammoth scale that the civilian private sector would have found impossible to establish from its own traditional resources.

Other wartime contributions were made in communications, navigation, and radar technology, and improvements were achieved in piston engine technology that significantly increased engine limits and durability. One of the most significant

wartime developments was the introduction of the jet engine and advances in high-speed aerodynamics, principally in Britain and Germany.

Perhaps the war's most useful experience was showing thousands of U.S. pilots who had never before been abroad how the airliner had made accessible the remotest corners of the earth as routinely as flying from San Francisco to Chicago.

In the immediate postwar air transport world, the United States settled down to the duel of the piston liners between Douglas and Lockheed while Britain launched the jet age with the turboprop Vickers Viscount and the ill-fated DeHavilland Comet. Overshadowed by the Comet's tragic series of crashes and loss of preeminence to the Boeing 707, the Viscount deserves greater recognition. It was the clear leader in the turboprop arena and served with distinction in relatively large numbers in the United States with Continental, United, and Northeast.

The late 1940s saw the introduction of the VOR navigation system and the commitment to the instrument landing system (ILS). The first onboard weather radar made its appearance in 1955. In 1956 a tragic collision over the Grand Canyon between a United DC-7 and a TWA Constellation led to the establishment of positive control airspace above 18,000 feet, requiring all aircraft to be on IFR flight plans and under the positive control of air traffic controllers.

When the jet age came to America's airlines, the issue was the need for more power. Engine makers were incessantly badgered for greater thrust. The first jets needed to have water injected into their engines to cool the airflow and make it denser so that sufficient thrust could be developed to get airborne. The problem was solved even before the first jets were introduced, but the airlines wouldn't think of waiting and running the risk of being scooped. The solution was the fan-jet that used part of the turbine's energy to turn a shrouded propeller-like fan to generate extra thrust efficiently.

Further progress into the widebody era was incremental. The Boeing 747 was massive, but technologically it was just a larger, fatter 707 or Super DC-8. As other aircraft preceding it, the 747 was put into service with engines that could barely meet its power needs, but engine upgrades soon solved the problem. Once the astonishment at its immense size abated, the most striking aspect about it was that no leading edge technology had to be cracked to build it. That is surely the industry's most convincing symbol of success.

A whole bagful of Caribbean bargains

(Like Puerto Rico for $122. Jamaica for $159. Antigua for $195. Barbados for $229.)

By the late 1960s, airborne mass tourism was soaring, bargain tickets abounded, and the decorum in the cabin was far less formal than a decade before. The possession of a Pan American bag was a fashion statement, implying exotic foreign travel by its owner.

Opposite: This stunt with the prototype Boeing 707 above Boeing's president, Bill Allen, and an assembly of dignitaries watching a hydrofoil race left Allen speechless. But despite the spectacular effect, the load on the airplane remained an even positive one G all the way around the roll. "The airplane never knew it was upside down," explained Boeing's flamboyant test pilot Tex Johnson, and he kept his job.

CHAPTER 2

American

The silver airliner being readied for departure at Chicago's Midway airport on June 25, 1936, was bigger than any airplane most of the assembled spectators had ever seen. Its sleek, futuristic airframe sported a sparkling polished metal finish adorned by the orange-and-blue lightning bolt trim line and logo of American Airlines. The dark blue letters on its nose identified it as the *Flagship Illinois*.

It was one of American Airlines' first DC-3s, a Douglas Sleeper Transport (DST) equipped with convertible sleeping berths for night travel, and it was about to make history. Its departure for New York was the first scheduled passenger flight of a DC-3, the airplane that would transform air transportation from an unpredictable adventure into a viable industry by enabling the airlines to provide safe, fast, and reliable passenger service at a profit.

Only one of the 14 passengers onboard the *Flagship Illinois* hadn't paid for his ticket. He was a tall, tough Texan wearing a trademark straw hat, and he was in an exceptionally jovial mood. He was Cyrus Rowlett Smith, president of American Airlines, but everyone just called him C. R. or Mr. C. R. He had single-handedly cajoled Donald Douglas into building the DC-3 when Douglas could barely keep up with orders for the airliner that had everyone else star-struck, the equally sleek but smaller, less capable DC-2.

When the *Flagship Illinois* landed in Newark 3 hours and 55 minutes after its midday departure from Midway, it had set a new record on the route and had launched the era of modern air travel. It also got a jump on the competition, beating United, the next DC-3 customer, by several months.

American Airlines had come far from beginnings that were not nearly as sure winged as the *Flagship Illinois'* flight to Newark. Its roots reach back to a hodgepodge of small airlines collected by Aviation Corporation (Avco), a holding company established in 1929 by W. A. Harriman & Company and Lehman Brothers to build an aviation conglomerate.

Avco controlled 13 airlines, some of which were controlled by holding companies of their own prior to joining the Avco conglomerate. With them came a patchwork of 11 air mail routes. Among the airlines swept up by Avco's acquisition frenzy was Embry Riddle; Universal Airlines System, which controlled six Midwest-based airlines including Robertson; Boston-based Colonial Airways; Southern Air Transport, which controlled St. Tammany Gulf Coast Airways and Texas Air Transport; and Interstate Airlines, which held the Chicago-Atlanta mail route.

Several achievers who worked for these airlines would figure prominently in the history of the U.S. airline industry. Robertson employed Charles Lindbergh, who flew the company's first scheduled air

American Airlines launched America's first transcontinental jet service with the Boeing 707 on January 25, 1959, slashing in half the DC-7's crossing time. American's initial 707 order was for 25 aircraft, shortly followed by an order for another 25 with more powerful fan-jet engines.

The Stinson Model A was one of many types in American's mixed fleet, which needed rationalization. It was a difficult task because American was stitched together from many small airlines that continued to operate autonomously for several years.

The Curtiss Condor was the first attempt at fleet rationalization. It was acquired for American's transcontinental route and was the airline's first sleeper plane, equipped with berthable seats and overhead berths. It was comfortable, but underpowered and its engines' propensity to catch fire prompted American to equip it with the first in-flight engine fire extinguishers on an aircraft.

C. R. Smith, American's president (left of the propeller blade) helps inaugurate DC-3 service on June 25, 1936, with the Flagship Illinois, about to depart Chicago for New York. C. R. coaxed the DC-3 out of Douglas in a marathon phone call.

mail flight on April 15, 1926, from St. Louis to Chicago. American's more enthusiastic fans like to claim that this flight made Lindbergh American's first pilot. One of Colonial's founders was Juan Trippe who went on to found Pan American and run it for four tumultuous decades. And Southern Air Transport's bookkeeper and operations manager was C. R. Smith, an accountant by training who got into the airline business when his boss at Texas-Louisiana Power Company gained control of Southern Air Transport and asked him to keep an eye on it.

A notable achievement during this period was the first transcontinental airline-train service established by Universal Air Transport in June 1929, between New York and Los Angeles, using Fokker F-10 Trimotors. It was novel but only marginally effective, with one flying leg between Cleveland and Garden City, Kansas. It shortened the trip by only about five hours compared to the best train schedules. Within a month Transcontinental Air Transport, which would become TWA, initiated a more effective air/rail service with two flying legs, shaving 20 hours off the fastest train crossings.

Avco's unwieldy airline holdings were losing money and were proving tough to manage, mixed in with another 70+ nonairline ventures, so on January 25, 1930, they were consolidated into a separate subsidiary. The new company was named American Airways.

It was a good first step, but even though the new entity was organized into Universal, Colonial, and Southern Air Transport divisions, they carried on as before, different fiefdoms flying different equipment in different directions. Their only common characteristic was their ability to continue losing money. But they formed one of the biggest airline conglomerates, and as Postmaster General Walter Folger Brown set out to reshape the U.S. airline industry

Part of American's DC-3 fleet that includes both sleepers and day-only aircraft lined up in a semicircle. American had a temporary advantage over the other airlines as the DC-3 launch customer with a big order and made the most of it.

under the sweeping powers granted him by the Watres-McNary Act of 1930, American Airways found that size matters.

At the infamous spoils conferences of 1930 that established three transcontinental routes American Airways ended up with the southern route and found itself one of the Big Four airlines controlling 90 percent of the nation's air traffic. The three others were the newly formed TWA on the central route and United on the northern route, and Eastern Air Transport.

Here was a chance to start stemming the flow of red ink, but half-hearted efforts to consolidate the

American Airlines' Douglas Sleeper Transports, the sleeper version of the DC-3, crossed the continent in three stops. Mercury Service passengers could leave New York in the late afternoon and be in Los Angeles by the following morning.

acquisitions threatened to dilute his holdings, he decided to act in characteristic fashion. He mounted a proxy fight for control of the airline and won.

Cord liked C. R. Smith, who had risen to head the Southern division and was made operations manager for all of American Airways just before the proxy fight. With Cord's support, Smith made his first significant decision on behalf of American Airways, the purchase of 10 Curtiss Condor sleeper airplanes.

It was an astute move in spite of the fact that from a technical perspective the Condor was a flop. A huge, pot-bellied, fabric-covered, strut-braced biplane at a time when all-metal monocoque airframes and cantilever wings were pointing the way to the future, it was woefully underpowered and especially vulnerable to icing. But its fat fuselage provided a hitherto unknown level of passenger luxury, and American Airways made the most of it by installing 14 sleeping berths that brought train-style overnight comfort, furthering the attraction of transcontinental air service and handsomely upstaging United and TWA.

With the introduction of the Condor sleepers in 1933, American hired its first stewardesses. The first class of four was sent on the line after only three days of training. All were registered nurses, a requirement that was to last until World War II.

Just as American was beginning to make a name for itself, especially under C. R. Smith's able management of the Southern division, the entire industry was hit by the cancellation of all air mail contracts following Congressman Hugo Black's charges of anticompetitive collusion at the spoils conferences. When the Army's attempt to fly the mail ended in disaster and the airlines were reawarded the mail routes in a new round of bidding under the Air Mail Act of 1934, American Airways came out of it with its route structure intact. It was renamed American Airlines to comply with the government's requirement it be a different company from the one that participated in the spoils conferences.

Concurrently, C. R. Smith became president of American Airlines. The stage was now set to complete American's consolidation and realize its potential. But immediately Smith faced exter-

American started the custom of putting out the airline's flag on its flagships, as it called its aircraft, for arrivals and departures. Many flags got mangled and lost in the slipstream when the pilots forgot to retrieve them before takeoff.

airline had little effect. Avco continued acquiring airlines, including Century Airlines and Century Pacific Airlines, both owned by E. L. Cord, a tough, tight-fisted entrepreneur, best known for his controlling interest in the Auburn Motor Company, who gained a seat on the Avco board.

As a major shareholder, Cord took a deep interest in American Airways and didn't like what he saw. He rightly felt that the company should be more integrated and better managed. When additional

American Airlines provided connecting service for passengers of the Hindenburg airship's transatlantic service arriving and departing from Lakehurst, New Jersey, commemorated in this baggage sticker.

The Douglas DC-4 was American's first four-engined airliner; an eagerly awaited interim airplane until the arrival of the pressurized DC-6.

nal threats to American's obsolete fleet. United had just introduced the Boeing 247, and TWA was inaugurating its first DC-2s. Although American Airlines also had 15 DC-2s on order, for the moment it was facing this formidable lineup with its tired Ford and Stinson Trimotors and the lumbering Condors. But C. R. Smith was already looking beyond the DC-2.

Firmly convinced of the need for an airliner that could make money without a mail subsidy, Smith and his chief engineer, Bill Littlewood, recognized that in the DC-2 for the first time they had an airplane that could be scaled up to realize this goal. Their figures showed that a 21-seat Douglas could turn a profit without the mail. In addition, C. R. wanted a sleeper version that could carry 14 berths in Condor style.

It is said that the usually monosyllabic Smith talked a reluctant Donald Douglas into building the DC-3 in a marathon $335.50 phone call. Douglas, who had his hands full with the DC-2, finally gave in when Smith committed to buying 20 DC-3s on the spot.

The first DST sleeper service was introduced on September 18, 1936, between Los Angeles and New York. The trip was completed in about 16 hours eastbound and 18 hours westbound with three refueling stops. On American's popular Mercury Service, passengers could leave Newark late in the afternoon, slip into their berths after dinner, and be in Los Angeles by morning.

With the DC-3, American embarked on an era of expansion that would make it America's biggest airline. Such ambitions required not only the world's best airplane, but impeccable and innovative service, objectives that the airline pursued with an obsession.

The DC-3s were designated flagships, and to properly live up to the name, American designed its own flag featuring four stars and the eagle. It was flown on the flagships during ground taxiing from a flagpole holder above the cockpit.

The flagship concept spawned another innovation, the Admirals Club. At first, membership was simply an honorary recognition of frequent fliers selected at the airline's discretion and presented with a colorful certificate. But when La Guardia Field opened in 1939, American opened the first of many Admiral's Club lounges.

American Overseas Airlines, majority owned and managed by American Airlines flew the first scheduled landplane crossing of the Atlantic on October 24, 1945, as illustrated in this postcard when the *Flagship New England*, a C-54 converted to civilian use flew from Boston to London.

An American Airlines DC-6 sleeper on short final. The pressurized DC-6 was sorely needed when it entered service in 1947 to counter TWA's Constellations.

In 1936 American became the first airline to introduce hot food in flight, prompted by the desire to enhance DC-3 service. A set of thermos containers dispensed hot coffee and kept warm the hot chicken or beef put on board prior to departure.

Another American contribution to air travel was the introduction of a scheme to allow passengers to purchase tickets with an air travel scrip book or a debit card, a forerunner of the credit card. Money would be put on deposit with the airline and the passenger could draw against it with the card. It was designed for business travelers whose companies paid the deposits and authorized their employees to draw on them with their cards. To induce its customers to sign up was a 15 percent discount on tickets bought this way. The program was so successful that it was adopted industrywide in 1936.

To keep track of the reservations flooding in as traffic mushroomed, American created a central reservations operation called the Tiffany Desk, not after the jewelers, but the employee who devised it. It was a command post with a 100-line switchboard. The operators yelled out incoming requests to an adjacent area called Space Control, which had all available spaces charted. Runners would rush back from Space Control to the Tiffany Desk with cards

confirming reservations. The atmosphere was just like a commodities trading pit.

During this period, American Airlines also founded the nation's air traffic control system. As early as 1934, American took the initiative to establish an in-house method of flight following. Starting with Chicago, American devised a system to track all of its aircraft within 100 miles of the airport using radio communications and a huge map table on which a representation of each airplane was pushed around as the flights progressed. American invited all traffic in and out of Chicago to use the system, and soon established similar centers for Newark and Cleveland. The results were so impressive that in 1936, the U.S. government took over the system and gradually expanded it to cover the whole country.

The DC-3's economies of scale began to pay off almost immediately, but American couldn't afford to be complacent. Even as its DC-3s were entering service, TWA ordered six Boeing 307 Stratoliners,

A young model named Norma Jeane tries out a lower berth on an American Airlines DC-6 sleeper before she became better known as Marilyn Monroe.

In first class, Mercury Service dinner was an elegant affair, although the variety of food wasn't particularly exciting. Steak or chicken in various turbocharged guises seemed to show up with great frequency.

pressurized four-engined 33-seat airliners that could cross the continent in only two stops and were faster than the DC-3.

To step beyond the DC-3, American joined a consortium formed to provide part of the research and development funding for Douglas to design and build its own pressurized four-engined airplane, the DC-4. Other participants were United, Eastern, Pan American (which also bought three of the Stratoliners), and TWA. Just about the only thing the DC-4 proved was that it shouldn't be built, at which point it was redesignated the DC-4E (Experimental). It was underpowered and overweight. Douglas decided it would make more sense to build an interim simplified, unpressurized airplane. This airplane was the DC-4, technologically not much more than a scaled-up DC-3 on tricycle gear. But with 44 seats, it was a major step forward.

American was among the first to order the DC-4, but its introduction would be interrupted by global upheaval. Before the first one could be delivered, the United States entered World War II and all

DC-4s went into military service straight off the assembly line, designated as C-54s.

By the summer of 1942, American also had to give up 38 of its 79 DC-3s as well as its president. Mr. C. R. had become Colonel C. R., and deputy commander of Air Transport Command (ATC), a job he held until the end of the war, leaving the service as a major general.

American's drafted fleet and pilots did their share of transport flying primarily on the North and South Atlantic routes, and many of its stewardesses joined up as nurses, looking after their wounded passengers on med-evac flights. By the war's end American Airlines was second only to Pan American in number of ATC missions flown.

One of American Airlines' most memorable contributions to the war effort was helping out the Army Air Corps flying supplies and equipment from India to China over the Himalayas across the dreaded Hump. American's crews flew 12 C-87s on the route, B-24 Liberators converted to freighters. During their 90-day assignment, they set a record for tonnage

American Overseas Airlines began taking delivery of an order of 16 Stratocruisers shortly before its sale to Pan American was completed. Pan American integrated them into its own fleet of Stratocruisers. American Airlines didn't return to the international market for three decades after it sold AOA.

In some respects the DC-6 was a big step up from the DC-3 seen in the background. But technologically, apart from the pressurization, it could be thought of as a grown-up DC-3 on tricycle gear.

hauled and lost only two aircraft, one to weather and one to mechanical failure on takeoff.

During the war American Airlines became an international carrier, first with forays into Mexico and Canada, followed by the acquisition of American Export Airlines (AEA), which was the first company to crack Pan American's transoceanic monopoly. AEA was set up in 1939 by American Export Lines, the shipping company, to provide transatlantic flying boat service. The mood toward competition was changing in Washington as the industry matured, and in 1940 AEA won CAB approval to operate to Lisbon, Portugal. World War II interrupted AEA's European plans, but its three Vought Sikorsky VS-44 Excalibur flying boats served Foynes, Ireland, throughout the war, and the line even provided C-54 service to North Africa under an ATC contract.

But Pan American took umbrage to the interloper and fought it bitterly through the CAB appeals process. It won the argument that in

AMERICAN AIRLINES
FLAGSHIP
INFORMATION

America's Leading Airline

terms of competition legislation, a shipping company couldn't own an airline. American Export Lines could retain a passive minority investment in AEA but had to divest itself of control. The CAB, however, got back at Pan American for throwing its weight around. In July 1945, it approved the acquisition of majority control of AEA by American Airlines.

The new entity was renamed American Overseas Airlines (AOA), and it started operations with six C-54s inherited from the military at the end of AEA's ATC contract. When the postwar transatlantic routes were awarded by the CAB among Pan Am and newcomers AOA and TWA, AOA got joint authority with Pan Am to London and its own territory in Northern Europe. It got off to a quick start by scooping its rivals with the first scheduled landplane passenger service across the Atlantic. On October 24, 1945, an AOA C-54, the flagship *New England*, flew the airline's inaugural trip from Boston to London, opening a new era in transatlantic air travel. In less than a year, AOA was also operating a small fleet of speedy, pressurized 049 Constellations flown by both of its transatlantic competitors.

American was also anxious to restart normal service on the postwar home front. It rapidly began putting in service 52 DC-4s in addition to its DC-3s. The DC-4s, however, were no match for TWA's 049 Constellations, which Lockheed was contractually prohibited by TWA from selling to transcontinental competitors. Douglas was somewhat late in responding with the DC-6, which American and United desperately needed to battle the Connies, but the two airlines got a reprieve of sorts when the Constellation was grounded for 69 days in mid-1946.

American and co-launch customer United finally inaugurated DC-6 service in April 1947. The airplane proved to be a tough competitor for the 049 Constellation, beating it across the continent by about an hour. But like the Constellation, it suffered a mechanical setback that grounded it for four months when it was most needed.

First, a United DC-6 caught fire over Bryce Canyon and crashed as it desperately struggled to reach a small strip. No immediate reason for the cause was apparent. Seventeen days later, fire alarms went off in the cockpit of an American Airlines DC-6 out of San Francisco over Gallup, New Mexico. An aggressive emergency descent to the airport below got the airplane on the ground seconds before it would have been too late. Everyone got out of the blazing propliner as emergency crews managed to extinguish the fire and save the airplane for close inspection.

American was the first to use an electro-mechanical reservations system, the Reservisor, which could add or delete reservations with the push of two sets of buttons. Later the company worked with IBM to devise the Sabre reservations system, which became widely used in the entire travel industry.

The crew had been transferring fuel when the fire broke out. The investigation revealed that as some excess fuel was vented overboard at the end of the transfer (a normal event), it seeped along the wing's underside directly into the poorly positioned cabin heater air intake and ignited. American was hit hard by the subsequent grounding, for by then the DC-6s provided 50 percent of its seating capacity.

Another important postwar equipment decision was finding a replacement for the DC-3. Both Convair and Martin were planning to enter the market with powerful, modern twins that had twice the seating capacity. Convair's entry was pressurized while Martin's was designed to be pressurizable in future versions. American evaluated both entries and was instrumental in convincing Convair to alter its design to the airline's specifications, rewarding it with 100 orders for the airliner that came to be called the Convair 240. The first ones entered service a few months after the DC-6 and eventually 75 of them flew for American into the early 1960s.

American also upgraded the AOA fleet by ordering 16 Boeing 377 Stratocruisers to replace its DC-4s and Constellations to match Pan American's luxurious transatlantic service.

This large equipment acquisition program allowed American to be one of the first airlines to phase out the early propliners. The DC-4s were all gone by 1948, after just two years of service, and the last DC-3 was retired in 1949 after flying the line for 13 years. By contrast, United flew its last DC-3s into the 1960s.

American's massive equipment upgrade was expensive and the expected postwar traffic boom didn't materialize to support it, which placed the conservative airline under some financial pressure. It prompted C. R. Smith to make one of the rare strategic errors of his career. To raise additional cash, he sold American Overseas Airlines to Pan American, completing the transaction in 1950.

He didn't need to do it. American could have financed its needs. But like William "Pat" Patterson of United, he looked at the shambles Europe was in after the war and genuinely believed that traffic across the Atlantic wouldn't grow. He viewed AOA as a potentially costly distraction from American's much larger domestic bread-and-butter business and saw

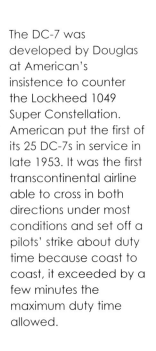

The DC-7 was developed by Douglas at American's insistence to counter the Lockheed 1049 Super Constellation. American put the first of its 25 DC-7s in service in late 1953. It was the first transcontinental airline able to cross in both directions under most conditions and set off a pilots' strike about duty time because coast to coast, it exceeded by a few minutes the maximum duty time allowed.

This collection of memorabilia commemorates American's transition from piston power to jets. The spark plug encased in lucite is from the last American Airlines piston aircraft to retire. *Martin Berinstein*

The water wagon 707 on takeoff trailing the tell-tale plume of smoke. The first 25 American Airlines 707s came with the less powerful engines that had to have water injected into the combustion chamber on takeoff. It cooled the air and made it more dense to pack a bigger punch when burned. A subsequent order for 25 additional 707s was for the later, fan-jet-equipped model, and the early 707s were also retrofitted with fan-jets.

no sense in holding on to it. American would be shut out of Europe for three decades.

In the meantime, Lockheed introduced the 749 Constellation to give the edge back to TWA over the DC-6. Douglas responded with the DC-6B, which became the most economical piston propliner ever built. American bought 25 DC-6Bs, putting the first ones on the line in 1951.

Airline services were expanding and changing rapidly as the 1940s gave way to the 1950s, and American played its customary leading role. Its most significant innovation was the family fare, which allowed family members to accompany the primary ticketholder at a 50 percent discount during mid-week travel. It was solid additional income to the airline because its users would have stayed off the airplanes at full fares, and the airline had sufficient excess capacity to accommodate them at the reduced fare. The concept was adopted industrywide.

American was also quick to offer coach services, introducing them in 1948 only a month after Capital started the trend. Air coach, as it was called, became a real money-maker, compensating for the reduced fares with higher volume.

As America's biggest airline, American continuously faced its greatest challenge in maintaining an efficient reservations system that tracked availability to the minute nationwide. The Tiffany Desk of the 1930s had been innovative for its time, but by the second half of the 1940s passenger traffic had increased fivefold, demanding a faster system.

The Tiffany Desk's successor was the Reservisor, devised by one of American's gadget-minded employees during World War II and introduced in 1946. It was the first electro-mechanical reservation system that allowed agents throughout the country to add reservations with one set of buttons and free up space with another. It was the ancestor of the computerized Sabre reservation system of the 1960s, which became one of American's most lucrative assets and was expanded to cover the entire industry and made accessible to travel agents nationwide.

An important development of the 1950s was the establishment of several interline agreements with other carriers to allow service without a change of planes through the participants' adjacent territory. As the aircraft worked its way across an interline route, it was flown within each airline's segment by its respective crews. American was an ideal interline partner for smaller carriers because of its long-range routes spanning the continent. Agreements were established with Delta, National, Braniff, and Continental to the West Coast.

Significant route awards during the 1950s included Chicago–San Francisco nonstop and New York–Houston via Pittsburgh and Nashville. The former enabled American to compete more effectively from New York to San Francisco, shortening the previous service through Dallas. But most of the new routes at this time were going to the smaller carriers as CAB sought to increase competition, judging the industry to be strong enough to take it.

In early 1951, American Airlines was responsible for convincing a reluctant Douglas Aircraft to build the initial version of its last great propliner, the DC-7. In Britain, the Comet jetliner was already flying. Many industry executives were of the opinion that jets were only a matter of time, and until then the excellent, efficient DC-6B would be sufficient to do the job. But C. R. Smith wasn't one of them. He was concerned about TWA's Lockheed Super G Constellation and reasoned

that an equal competitor was worth the expense to protect market share even if it was an interim airplane. His clout with Douglas won the debate.

The DC-7 was troublesome because of its cantankerous, over-boosted Curtiss Wright R-3350 turbo-compound engines that failed with annoying regularity. The frequent and expensive unscheduled engine maintenance made it considerably less profitable than the DC-6B. Nevertheless, it was the first airliner capable of nonstop transcontinental crossings in both directions, completing the trip in just over eight hours depending on winds aloft, and racked up a perfect safety record with American in a decade of service.

American acquired 25 DC-7s and inaugurated nonstop coast-to-coast Mercury Service with them in late 1953, followed by Royal Coachman coach service in 1956. Flights operated in all first class, all coach,

When the 707 (pictured) and 720 were introduced by American, the company confusingly called the 720s 707 Jet Flagships, presumably worried about an identity crisis caused by the difficulty of telling the difference between the two jets. Shortly thereafter, all flagships became Astrojets and the model designations were used to identify the different types.

and mixed class configurations. The CAB approved an exemption for transcontinental DC-7 cockpit crews from the eight-hour flight time limit to legalize flying the few extra minutes it took to complete the flights. This change led to a union-mandated pilot's strike, which was resolved by arbitration in American's favor. However, it caused some lingering tension between management and the pilots, which would become an increasingly more common phenomenon throughout the industry.

Six years after introducing the DC-7, American entered the jet age in characteristic fashion. On January 25, 1959, its first Boeing 707 launched the nation's first transcontinental jet service with a flight from Los Angeles to New York. It dramatically slashed in half the dethroned DC-7's crossing time.

The Boeing 707 was chosen over the DC-8 by American because it was available ahead of its rival. Initially, American was leaning strongly toward the DC-8 because Boeing wasn't willing to widen the 707 fuselage to accommodate six abreast seating. The tooling was ready and changing it would be expensive. However, pressure from the airlines mounted for the change. Pan American, the 707's launch customer, shocked Boeing by concurrently ordering a larger number of DC-8s primarily because of the fuselage width issue. American then told Boeing that it would not order the airplane without the change, and Boeing, not wishing to duplicate the B-247's experience against the DC-2 and -3 wisely relented.

American's first 25 Boeing 707s were equipped with the JT-3 engine, the only powerplant available for them at the time. They left the aircraft underpowered and required water injection on takeoff, which cooled the air inflow and increased thrust. These early "water wagons" were followed by an order for another 25 Boeing 707s with the more powerful and fuel-efficient fan-jet engines that made the 707 so successful. In due course the initial batch of 707s were retrofitted with fan-jets.

A beautiful portrait of a Boeing 720 acquired for medium-haul routes to complement the Boeing 707s. The 720 was a quick fix for the medium-haul market, derived from the 707, but different in more ways than may be superficially apparent. The wing was substantially redesigned, the airframe was significantly lightened, and there were some systems differences.

When American Airlines introduced its first Boeing 727 in 1964, the airline was once again operating a trimotor for the first time since it sold its last Ford Trimotors in the 1930s. The two types were brought together to commemorate the event.

Two days before the historic transcontinental 707 flight, the company inaugurated the first of 35 turboprop Lockheed Electras selected for its medium-haul routes. The Electra was an easier choice, made urgent by the clobbering Capital Airlines' turboprop Vickers Viscounts were giving American's piston liners on its lucrative eastern routes.

Shortly after its first 707 order, American also ordered 10 shorter-range Boeing 720s, positioned between the 707 and the Electra. The 720 shared common elements with the 707, but it was a highly modified version with different wings and some different systems. Confusingly, American called its 720 the 707 (Model 720) Jet Flagship. American was the first to inaugurate 720 service in July 1960, with a flight from Cleveland to Los Angeles via St. Louis. The route was typical of the stage lengths for the 707. Concurrent with the second round of 707 fan-jet orders, American also ordered 15 additional fan-jet-powered 720s.

With the introduction of the fan-jets, the venerable Flagship name that first adorned the DC-3s was retired. American renamed all of its jets Astrojets,

Following Braniff's lead in search of a short-haul twinjet, American purchased a fleet of BAC 111-400s. They were known as 400 Astrojets and were more powerful than Braniff's 111s. They entered service in 1965 and were eventually replaced by Boeing 727-200s.

implying a link to the brave new space frontier. Speed was still king, and its quest prompted American to select the Convair 990, which promised to be the fastest Astrojet. It proved to be C. R. Smith's only poor equipment decision.

A scaled-up version of the Convair 880 ordered by TWA and Delta, the CV 990 was smaller than the 707 and featured five-abreast seating. In spite of Convair's best efforts, its airframe drag was higher than promised and it missed guaranteed speed performance and burned more fuel than projected. American cut back its order of 25 to 20.

Though a disappointment, the Convair 990s ably served American's thinner medium-haul routes at 707 speeds from 1962 to 1968.

Next on American's jet agenda was finding a short-haul pure jet to replace the turboprops, and a more versatile successor for the Boeing 720s. The two types the company bet on were the British Aircraft Corporation BAC 111 and the Boeing 727. The 727 was ordered first and put in service in early 1964. Economical on routes as short as 150 miles and as long as 2,000 miles, and able to operate from 5,000-foot runways, it became one of air transportation's

biggest success stories, especially the stretched 727-200 series. American got its first 200s in 1968, and they went on to form the majority of the airline's fleet through the 1980s.

Being the best alternative at the time, the British short-haul twinjet BAC 111 was selected in 1963 with an order for 15 aircraft followed up by an additional 15. It was a more advanced version of the 111s flown by Braniff and regional Mohawk, and was called the 400 Astrojet after its model designation. It entered service with American in 1966 and the following year even competed with the Eastern Shuttle as the Jet Express. Not organized to provide guaranteed seats to all comers without reservations, the Jet Express was not as successful as had been hoped and was wound up. On other routes, the 111s were eventually superceded by the growing fleet of Boeing 727s.

In 1966, American introduced youth fares to tap the growing number of student travelers in an increasingly affluent society. It was another innovation accepted industrywide.

Astrovision and Astrocolor were introduced to provide in-flight entertainment. Astrovision was a television system that showed passengers the take-offs and landings with a nose-mounted camera and could also show movies in-flight. Astrocolor followed TWA's lead in presenting in-flight movies and was the first color projection system designed specifically for use in aircraft.

Less popular at American was an attempt to ditch the eagle logo in an otherwise attractive new color scheme proposed by designer Henry Dreyfuss to replace the blue-and-international-orange livery barely modified since DC-3 days. A "save the eagle" campaign was successful and at the end of the 1960s, the new, modified livery was applied and would fly into the twenty-first century.

As the 1970s got underway, the rescued eagle was about to soar on the tail of the biggest American airliner, the Boeing 747. American joined the pack with a large order for the giant jet, intending to use it on transcontinental routes. But the mid-sixties' breathless projections of soaring passenger traffic that prompted the deal didn't materialize, and the 747s flew with dismally small passenger loads. To transform the cavernous, deserted cabins into friendlier spaces, American installed coach lounges in addition to first class lounges and created a famous Wurlitzer piano bar where entertainers travelling with the airline were welcome to give impromptu performances.

But the 747s were not an entirely lost cause. In 1969, American won rights to serve Hawaii from various mainland destinations and slowly they found their calling serving the islands. They were also increasingly promoted as LuxuryLiners.

In 1969, American also became an international airline once again, three decades after it sold American Overseas Airlines. It won rights to serve the South Pacific and Australia. The company was hoping to get access to the far more lucrative Tokyo market, so its elevation to international status was somewhat of a letdown. Nevertheless, the thinly traveled South Pacific routes proved useful when they were later traded with Pan American for Caribbean destinations. They strengthened the Puerto Rico-centered route structure American acquired in 1971 when it bought out Trans Caribbean Airways.

American's big contribution to the widebody era was launching the McDonnell Douglas DC-10. American's chief engineer believed that the 747 was too big for its transcontinental routes and such high density sectors as the Chicago–New York route, preferring a 250-passenger twin-aisle aircraft instead. The choice came down to two highly similar aircraft, the DC-10 and the Lockheed L-1011. Wary of Lockheed's lack of jetliner experience and reassured by McDonnell Corporation's bailout of Douglas in spite of massive production problems with the DC-8 and DC-9 lines, American opted for the DC-10, along with United, which had a strong preference for the airplane's GE engines over the Rolls-Royce of the L-1011.

American signed up for 25 DC-10s and 25 options in 1968 and inaugurated DC-10 service in August 1971 on the Chicago–Los Angeles run. The DC-10 lived up to its promise, but shortly after it entered service it got a black eye because of a badly designed cargo door latching mechanism. Inadvertently unlatched cargo doors caused a nearly disastrous decompression incident on an American DC-10, and a few months later brought down a Turkish Airlines aircraft. However, once the problem was fixed and less serious bugs worked out, the DC-10 became the workhorse of American's widebody fleet and lived on in the MD-11.

American managed to weather the recession of the early 1970s and the subsequent energy crisis, although, like the entire industry, it had to severely economize, reducing capacity and furloughing thousands of employees. When deregulation came, American was one of the winners. Ably led by Robert Crandall, a CEO every bit as tough and capable as the original Big Four titans, it expanded dramatically at home and overseas to grow into a financially robust major international airline that would greatly please Mr. C. R.

American Airlines became a Boeing 747 operator and suffered the consequences of a slump in traffic just as they were introduced. To fill up the empty spaces, American installed a Wurlitzer piano bar on some of its 747s. In the end they proved useful serving Hawaii and some were freighters, but the 747 was never a big component of American's fleet.

United

A two-way radio had recently been installed in the Pacific Air Transport Boeing 40 mail plane that Russ Cunningham was ferrying one New Year's Eve in the late 1920s from Seattle, Washington, to Medford, Oregon. He was visually following the flashing beacons set out every 25 miles to mark the airway, when the weather rapidly deteriorated and the ground began to fade out.

The traditional response would have been to descend to tree top level and struggle to visually maintain ground contact over the rugged mountains that had claimed the lives of so many of his friends. But Cunningham, who was one of the first converts to the idea of homing in on radio beams to guide aircraft in poor weather, decided to experiment. He started climbing to safely clear the surrounding ridges and listened to the Medford radio operator to fine tune his compass course by lining up in the direction of the loudest radio transmissions.

Approaching 12,000 feet, Cunningham encountered another potential killer. He picked up so much ice that his airplane could no longer maintain altitude. As the stricken Model 40 descended, he kept coolly shepherding it toward the loudest radio transmissions all the way down and pancaked into a patch of deep snow. Unhurt, he started to walk in the direction his radio had told him was toward

Medford and made it, only a day and a half late. Within a few years, airliners were routinely "riding the beam" of Morse-coded radio transmissions to find their way.

Cunningham, whose employer was one of four airlines that were joined to form United Airlines, exemplified the many forward-looking pilots, engineers, and technicians who earned United a reputation for being one of the technically most innovative U.S. airlines. He went on to become director of technical communications, and by the time he retired, United's first Douglas DC-8 jets were riding the beam nonstop across the continent in four and a half hours.

The moving force behind the airline that Cunningham would serve for so long was the Boeing Company, which, by the beginning of the 1930s had assembled around itself the biggest and one of the most successful aviation conglomerates in the United States. The four airlines, Boeing Air Transport, Pacific Air Transport, Varney Air Lines, and National Air Transport spanned the continent and were a captive market for the civilian aircraft it produced. The engine maker, Pratt & Whitney, was the source of its Wasp and Hornet powerplants. Hamilton Propeller Company supplied its propellers. All the companies, including the Boeing Company, were

United thought it had a major lead over the rest of the industry with the 60 Boeing 247s built for it by its sister company. But a small, Californian aircraft maker, inexperienced in modern all-metal construction, soon set back United's plans for the 247 and had it lining up within a few years for the DC-3.

be good enough to collar an order for 50 primary trainers from the U.S. Navy in 1917. Boeing was in the airplane business.

When World War I ended and military opportunities dried up, the fledgling company almost failed, pulling through only by turning to making furniture. The 1920s brought new military fighter contracts, but what Bill Boeing wanted was a civilian opportunity, and the 1925 Kelly Air Mail Act delivered it. Boeing and his associates shrewdly realized that the way to make money carrying the mail was to build a mail plane vastly superior to the gallant but aging World War I-inspired fleet available to the competition.

When the transcontinental air mail came up for bids in two segments on the San Francisco–Chicago–New York route, they were ready with the Boeing 40A biplane. Powered by the air-cooled Pratt & Whitney Wasp engine it could outrace and out-lift the competition by a large margin and even had a small, enclosed cabin for two to accommodate the handful of passengers foolhardy enough to insist going by air.

The Boeing Company won the San Francisco–Chicago segment of the transcontinental route by grossly underbidding Harris "Pop" Hanshue of Western Air Express, and formed Boeing Air Transport (BAT) to handle the new venture. BAT dubbed its route the Main Line and started service with the first of a fleet of 25 Boeing 40As in June 1927. It quickly proved wrong rampant rumors of its early demise. Instead of disappearing from the scene as fast as it had come, it was soon searching for additional opportunities and would get them by acquisition.

First to join the fold was Pacific Air Transport (PAT), acquired in January 1928. Founded in early 1926 by Vern Gorst, a former bus service operator hooked on aviation, PAT had won the Los Angeles–Seattle air mail route and valiantly operated it in spite of being perpetually underfunded. Help came in part from a rookie lender at Wells Fargo Bank named William "Pat" Patterson who had started as a messenger and worked his way up. Patterson made his first loan to Pacific Air Transport and was taken enough by the business to help it on his own time as an unpaid financial advisor.

By 1928 Patterson's advice was to sell out to Boeing, who paid a handsome premium to Gorst and other holders of PAT stock, including the madam of a North Bend, Oregon, brothel who had received two shares for services rendered.

Phil Johnson, president of both Boeing Air Transport and the Boeing Company liked what he saw in the youthful banker and convinced him to

The Boeing B-40 gave Boeing Air Transport the ability to haul mail profitably at half the price bid by the competition. Boeing realized that high performance was key to competing successfully with the war surplus DeHavillands powered by obsolete water-cooled Liberty engines. BAT could fly the mail at the low rates it bid because it didn't have to haul water and radiators.

held under the protective umbrella of a holding company, the United Aircraft and Transport Company. Soon they were joined by the Standard Steel Propeller Company, Northrop Aircraft, Sikorsky Airplane Company, and Stearman Aircraft.

It was a formidable empire that came into being because Bill Boeing, the man who started it all, loved to hunt and fish. A wealthy Seattle lumber heir, Boeing had wandered into the world of aviation in 1915 only because he was looking for a faster way to reach the prime hunting and fishing grounds of British Columbia, north of his hometown.

Boeing bought a Glenn Martin flying boat, but soon crashed the fragile sticks and wire craft. Frustrated by the long wait for replacement parts, he decided to build his own design, aided by a close friend, Commander Conrad Westervelt of the U.S. Navy. The B&W 1 flew much better than the original Glenn Martin. The design was further refined by MIT engineering graduate Wong Tsu and proved to

join Boeing as his assistant and to back up Edward Hubbard, the airline's executive vice president and general manager. When Hubbard unexpectedly passed away in the winter of 1929, the 29-year-old Pat Patterson was stunned to find himself appointed executive vice president and general manager. He would go on to run the airline for the next 36 years, capping off his career with a $750 million order for Boeing and Douglas jets.

By 1929, the passenger demand was sufficient on the San Francisco–Chicago route to justify the introduction of Boeing's first airliner, the Wasp-powered Trimotor Boeing 80. It carried 12 passengers at a stately 125 miles per hour and had a cabin interior as luxurious as a Pullman rail car. Wood paneling, plush upholstery, and Edwardian light fixtures cocooned the passengers from the elements at its typical cruising altitudes of 8,000–10,000 feet. Within a year, the 80 was upgraded to the 80A with more powerful Hornets, which allowed for up to 18 passengers. In all, 15 Boeing 80s served BAT.

The Model 80 and Boeing Air Transport claimed the honor of introducing the first stewardesses. The idea was the brainchild of Ellen Church, a registered nurse from San Francisco with a passion to fly. She convinced the company that a registered nurse on each passenger flight would give a psychological boost to the typically apprehensive passenger's state of mind as well as provide food and beverage service and look after their general comfort. Church was appointed chief stewardess, and she recruited seven colleagues for the first class. They flew for the first time in May 1930 and launched a new profession.

The next company to join the fold was Stout Air Services in 1929 that served the Midwest. The following year, United Aircraft acquired the company that transformed Boeing Air Transport into a transcontinental airline and merged Stout with its earlier acquisition. It was National Air Transport (NAT), operator of the lucrative Chicago–New York air mail route, and it was literally wrestled away in a vicious stock battle from the group controlled by Clement Keys, which also owned Transcontinental Air Transport (TAT) and Eastern Air Transport. Boeing won the battle for NAT in May 1930, and by then it was close to acquiring Varney Air Lines, the final piece of United's budding airline empire.

The Boeing B-80 Trimotor was Boeing's first multi-engined airliner produced in quantity. It flew with United and its predecessor companies until replaced by the Boeing 247. The opulent wood-paneled interior was reminiscent of a Victorian parlor. The first stewardesses in America, hired by United in 1930, earned their wings on the B-80.

Founded by Walter Varney in 1925, Varney Air Lines appeared to be the airline that went nowhere, initially holding the air mail route between Pasco, Washington, and Elko, Nevada, via Boise, Idaho. Elko was soon changed to Salt Lake City, neatly connecting to the Main Line at a population center. By 1929, it had pushed on beyond Pasco to Seattle. Varney, a flamboyant wheeler-dealer, had bid the isolated route because he rightly assumed that he would win it with a high bid, and shrewdly deducted the advantage of connecting to the transcontinental route. Varney ran a good show, but like many of his peers, he was perpetually undercapitalized and sold out to escape a mountain of debt.

With the Varney acquisition in June 1930, United Aircraft and Transport Company's four airlines formed the strongest air transport company in the business, responsible for carrying 75 percent of the nation's air mail and providing 33-hour coast-to-coast passenger service.

United's position was further strengthened in 1930 by the Watres-McNary Act that changed the mail rate from payment per pound carried to payment per unit of air mail carrying capacity provided by the carrier. This legislation tended to encourage the larger airlines to make an increased commitment to carrying the mail and drove the small operators out of business.

The act also gave Postmaster General Walter Folger Brown sweeping powers to structure the carriage of the air mail as he saw fit. And he saw fit to award the transcontinental business to three of the strongest airlines to build a viable air transport industry. United retained its routes, TAT became TWA and got the central route, and American Airways got the southern route. Combined with Eastern Air Transport who got a near-monopoly on the East Coast's north-south routes, the four airlines between them accounted for 95 percent of the U.S. airline business.

United's share was over 40 percent, but it wanted more. It made a move to acquire Eastern Air Transport (EAT) in a proxy fight similar to its battle to acquire NAT, but Postmaster Brown would have none of it. He had his own limit to how large any one airline should get to maintain his idea of managed competition, and United had breached it. Brown ordered United to divest EAT stock, and the status quo was restored.

Boeing Air Transport was one of four predecessor companies from which United was formed. The others were National Air Transport, Pacific Air Transport, and Varney. Until 1934 they operated as independent subsidiaries and together they spanned the continent.

An enthusiastic crowd watches the Boeing 247, the revolutionary new aviation industry's latest marvel in this airport scene.

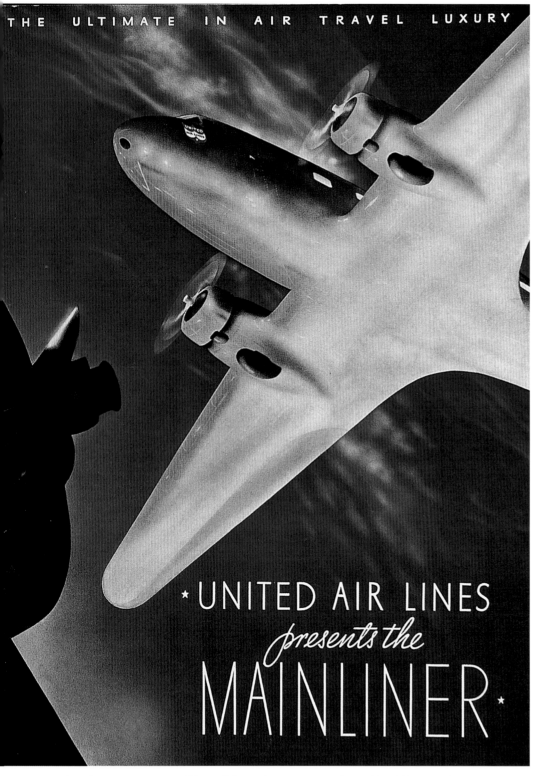

★ UNITED AIR LINES
presents the
MAINLINER ★

A pleasing art deco rendition of the DC-3 captures the spirit of flight as felt in the 1930s.

For United, it was time to digest its acquisitions and rationalize its organization to plan for a bright future. In 1931, its four airlines were placed under a management company named United Airlines and began doing business under that name although retaining their own, separate incorporation. The management company gave the airlines a new, common identity but owned nothing and made no payments.

United's next step was to introduce a revolutionary new airliner, the Boeing 247, which represented a quantum leap beyond the Fokker, Ford, and Stinson Trimotors and the twin-engined Curtiss Condor that dominated the equipment scene. The 247 turned out to be a fine airliner, but it would be badly upstaged by another pair, the DC-2 and its larger sibling, the DC-3.

The 247 could have been more competitive with the new Douglas airliners, but for once the airline's inherent conservatism worked to its disadvantage. Boeing proposed a 16,000-pound airliner equipped with the new, more powerful Hornet engines, but the pilots doubted whether such a large aircraft could be safely operated from the fields along their routes. They also strongly preferred the less powerful but tried-and-true Wasp engines to the unproven Hornets. The design was scaled down to the 10-passenger, 12,000-pound Boeing 247, and construction began in 1932.

United agreed to take 60 Boeing 247s, a staggering order even by today's standards, and put the first ones in service in June 1933. Preceding the DC-2s by a year, they were an instant hit throughout the industry. Their 160 miles per hour cruising speed topped their fastest competitors by 40 miles per hour and reduced coast-to-coast travel time by a third to just under 20 hours. But disaster was around the corner, not in the form of competition or a crash, but government action. President Roosevelt's trust-busting Democratic administration cancelled all the air mail contracts alleging collusion at Walter Folger Brown's 1930 spoils conferences, and handed over responsibility for flying the mail to the U.S. Army.

United, the country's biggest airline, had the resources to make a stand. It defiantly continued to fly its schedules, losing a million dollars in the four months it took the administration to recognize that the Army wasn't equipped to handle the mail and reverse its decisions. Equally worrisome for United was the cheeky flight made by TWA's Jack Frye and Eastern's Eddie Rickenbacker in the DC-1 to make a point with TWA's last transcontinental mail load before the ban came into effect. They crossed the continent in the Boeing 247's soon-to-be arch rival in 13 hours and 4 minutes.

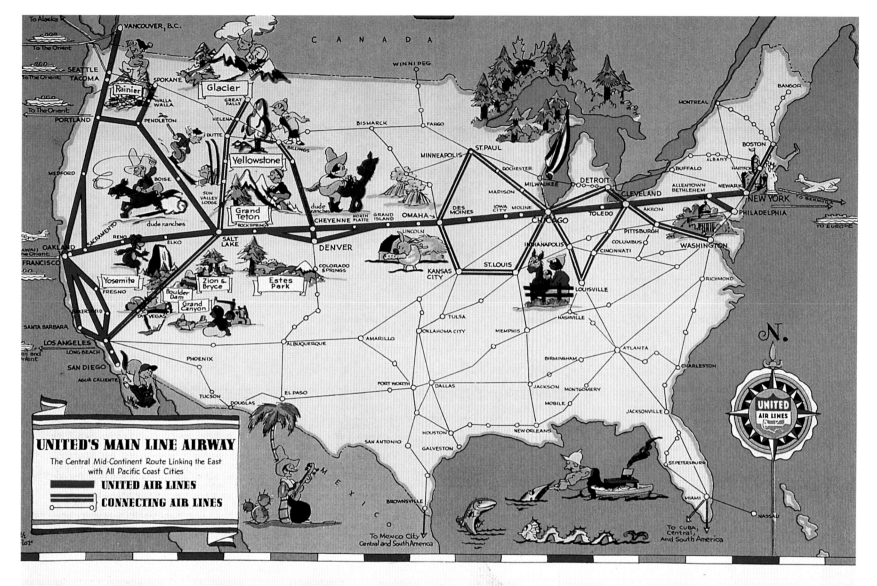

FLYING UNITED'S MAIN LINE AIRWAY

When the mail routes were returned to the airlines under the Air Mail Act of 1934, United regained all of its routes except the Chicago-Dallas leg, which went to Braniff. Because its four component airlines were still independent legal entities and the airlines that participated in the spoils conferences theoretically couldn't regain their routes, United incorporated all of them under the United Airlines management company and effectively carried on as before.

The biggest change brought about by the 1934 Air Mail Act for United was an enforced divorce from its non-airline sister companies in the breakup of United Aircraft and Transport Company. On anticompetitive grounds, the act decreed an end to the

giant aviation conglomerates with a self-serving finger in every pie. United Aircraft and Transport Company separated into the Boeing Airplane Company, Pratt & Whitney, and United Airlines. It was a good move for United, allowing the airline to break free from the pressures of choosing in-house equipment to conduct its business.

One United casualty of the 1934 Air Mail Act was Phil Johnson, barred from the aviation industry because of his participation in the spoils conferences. Pat Patterson, who hadn't been a participant and had become president of United Airlines in 1933 was determined to vindicate his former boss. He sued the government to reclaim $3.1 million lost

A United route map brochure from the 1930s covers the entire country in a series of highly detailed, colorful cartoons that gave passengers a lot to discover if they got bored en route.

The pilots got all the glory in the public's eye but equal credit belonged to the many mechanics who kept the airliners flying and expeditiously and reliably dealt with the many quirks of engines and systems that pushed the limits of the day's technology.
Martin Berinstein

in revenue because of the wrongful cancellation of the air mail contracts.

The Long Suit, as the case came to be known, dragged on until 1943, when a token award in favor of United at last formally vindicated Johnson's reputation, long after he had been allowed to return to head the Boeing Company. But Patterson's principled stand had a business cost. The government was so irked by the suit that for its duration, it denied any meaningful new route awards to the airline.

During the second half of the 1930s, United focused on developing its substantial territory and maximizing the advantages of the Main Line, the shortest route between California and the East Coast. The biggest problem confronting the airline in the mid-1930s was the debut of the DC-2 and DC-3. Passengers deserted United's Boeing 247s in droves for the Douglas liners, especially on the lucrative and competitive Chicago–New York run which they could fly nonstop. United had no choice but to throw in the towel with a massive DC-3 order of its own. It had to get in line behind TWA, American, and Eastern, but by the end of 1936 deliveries began and within a year, 29 DC-3 Mainliners, including DST sleeper versions, were flying in United colors. The airline's pre-war DC-3 fleet eventually grew to 57 aircraft.

But the Boeing 247s didn't go to waste. They migrated to the system's lower-density feeder routes where they served for years as ably as the Lockheed L-10 Electras that were coming into service.

Although United's passenger figures steadily rose, it lost some ground to the competition primarily because of its inability to win new routes in the East. Its system, while impressive in terms of route mileage, served areas of low population density. As other airlines grew faster by adding new population centers to their routes, United's total share of passenger traffic eroded from 44 percent in 1934 to 23 percent in 1937 when American overtook it as the nation's largest airline.

But United remained a colossus in an optimistic, if financially volatile business, and enthusiastically embraced new, innovative concepts to convert the public to going by air. Patterson took a leading role in convincing the entire industry to adopt and make interchangeable among all airlines American's air travel scrip books that offered a 15 percent discount.

United originated the first two-for-one ticket by allowing wives to fly free to accompany their husbands on business trips. A spouse's complementary first taste of air travel went a long way to encourage family pleasure travel in coming years.

The company also introduced Skylounge flights on the Chicago–New York route, which was arguably the first first-class airline service. For a two-dollar surcharge on a $26 ticket, passengers flew in a DC-3 with only 14 swivel chairs, seven in a single row on each side of the cabin. But the ticket surcharge wasn't sufficient to offset the revenue lost by the seven seats that had to be removed from the standard configuration. The service lost money and was soon discontinued.

Another United innovation was the first airline flight kitchen established in Oakland, California, in 1936. Run by Swiss chefs and expanded to strategic locations throughout the system, it took airline food out of the creamed-chicken-in-a-thermos-jug era as advances in galley design were about to make top restaurant-quality meals aloft a reality.

An interesting United experiment in 1940 was an interchange agreement with Western Airlines. It jointly operated a DST sleeper from Chicago to Los Angeles via Salt Lake City, where the crews would switch to fly their respective airline's segment. After World War II, such agreements became widespread.

Another novel service was the first shuttle, between San Francisco and Los Angeles, flown by Boeing 247s. It was quite successful, but was stopped by the war.

United's Skylounge passengers ride in the quiet atmosphere of a club lounge, and enjoy the spaciousness and extra luxury of fourteen deep-cushioned swivel chairs in a cabin large enough for 21 ordinary seats.

Mainliner Meals

Prepared by
SCHOOL AND COLLEGE SERVICE
of
UNITED AIR LINES

Arguably, United was first with first class when it created the luxurious Skylounge flights between Chicago and New York. For an extra $2 on a $26 ticket, passengers could fly in 14-seat Skylounge comfort. But the service missed the DC-3's point. It couldn't make money with 14 seats even with the surcharge, and the service was short-lived.

United was the first airline to have its own flight kitchens. It started the first one in Oakland, California, in 1936, importing Swiss chefs for the experiment. It was successful and was rapidly expanded throughout the United network and later copied by other airlines.

The original Douglas DC-4 was an experiment funded in part by a United-led consortium of airlines in the late 1930s to develop the DC-3's pressurized replacement. The project reached too far and produced an overweight, underpowered triple-tailed aircraft that was abandoned in favor of a simpler, unpressurized, interim airplane that became the DC-4. Douglas applied the experience to the successful postwar DC-6.

Although the DC-3 was the first airliner to be able to turn a profit without a postal subsidy, it also showed that future profits lay in even larger aircraft. United took the lead in the development of a four-engined successor by under-writing half the development costs of a new Douglas project, the DC-4. Patterson, who strongly believed in strategic cooperation in the industry's interest, subsequently allowed American, TWA, Eastern, and Pan American to participate and share United's development costs.

The triple-tailed DC-4E (E for experimental) reached too far technologically and turned out to be overweight and underpowered. It first flew in mid-1938 and by the time United put it through a two-month route-proving run the following year, it became clear that a less ambitious step up from the DC-3 was the better option. The scaled-down airplane was the 44-passenger unpressurized DC-4 that would exponentially increase the industry's route coverage and passenger capacity, but would first earn its stripes in World War II as the C-54. And United would earn a few stripes of its own with it.

During World War II, U.S. airlines were drafted to turn the few adventurous, far-flung air routes that linked the continents with limited service into a global spider web that made flying anywhere in the world almost as routine as spanning the United States from coast to coast.

The World's Fairs were important events in the days when the media was less effective at inundating society with up-to-the-minute information, and aviation was a major feature. United had the unusual privilege of connecting the two cities sharing the World's Fair with its Mainline transcontinental service and capitalized on the opportunity.

United's major contribution was establishing regular transpacific service (along with Pan American) between the United States and Australia. The 8,269-mile route was first flown by C-87s and then by the C-54s that United had hoped to fly on the Main Line as the DC-4. By the war's end, when United's airplanes formed part of the massive air transport armada that landed in Japan on V-J Day, the company had completed more than 7,000 Pacific crossings with only three accidents.

United also provided service to Alaska, especially during the war's early phase, and its Wyoming maintenance base and Oakland mechanic training school made other important contributions.

As the war clouds cleared, several airlines competed intensely for international route awards as Pan American's monopoly began to crack, but United wasn't among them. In a rare misjudgment, Pat Patterson felt that the traffic volumes wouldn't justify more than one U.S. international carrier and turned United's attention to domestic expansion. One important postwar route award that was in part prompted by United's wartime service was authorization to serve Honolulu from San Francisco and shortly thereafter from Los Angeles. On the all-important densely populated East Coast, United gained access to Boston and Detroit among other destinations.

Like its competitors, United acquired surplus C-54s converted to DC-4 configuration for its long-range routes as quickly as they became available. By October 1945, the first DC-4s were put into service, and within two years, the fleet grew to 31 aircraft. But for transcontinental routes, the DC-4 was a stop-gap solution because even as they appeared, TWA was inaugurating the far superior pressurized Lockheed Constellation. The race was on to build the ultimate propliner and Douglas was playing catch up.

United regained its competitive edge in October 1946 with the first deliveries of the DC-6, Douglas' answer to the Constellation. Pressurized like its rival, the DC-6 was slightly faster and more economical to operate. By the time the DC-6 entered service, the Constellation had lost some of its head start by being grounded when a design fault that was difficult to trace set off an in-flight electrical fire that caused a crash.

But soon the DC-6 and United also suffered a tragic setback when a new DC-6 caught fire and crashed into Bryce Canyon with the loss of all on board. The cause wasn't uncovered until an American DC-6, which also caught fire, made a successful emergency landing and examiners traced the prob-

Boeing 247 vs. Douglas DC-3

The numbers tell the story of the DC-3's advantage over the Boeing 247. Both aircraft employed the same technology and Boeing had a head start. As the baggage labels reveal, the 247's biggest customer was quick to get in line for the DC-3. The number of DC-3s built includes the approximately 13,000 C-47s and DC-3s made for World War II.

	B-247 (1933)	DC-3 (1936)
Cruise Speed	160	180 (mph)
Range	500	500 (sm)
Gross Weight	13,650	25,200 (lbs)
Passengers	10	21
Number Built	75	13,500

Source: R. E. G. Davies, *Airlines of the United States Since 1914.*

lem to a fuel vent that routed fuel into a cabin heater. The grounding of the DC-6 until a fix was implemented was costly to all the airlines involved.

In 1947, United got a lucky break. It had coveted nonstop Denver–Los Angeles authority for years, but the award had gone to Western. Now Western was hard hit by the postwar slowdown in passenger traffic and needed to raise cash. It was willing to sell the Denver–Los Angeles route and United snapped it up. The next year the company solidified its Denver position by opening a main operations base there.

United's next equipment purchase following the DC-6 was motivated by competitive pressures on the Hawaiian routes. Honolulu service had been inaugurated in 1947 with DC-6s, but Pan American had plans to fly the plush Boeing 377 Stratocruiser to the islands and United couldn't afford to fall behind. The cavernous double-decker wasn't faster than the DC-6 but to passengers it was the last word in luxury. United ordered seven of the blunt-nosed giants and received them in 1949–1950.

The company wasn't entirely happy with the Stratocruisers because they were so expensive to fly and maintain that they made little or no money. By 1955 they all were gone, sold to Britain's state-owned international airline, BOAC, and were replaced by DC-7s, which were faster but also had their share of engine problems.

United was behind several of its contemporaries in finding a replacement for the DC-3, though not for lack of trying. It had gone as far as placing an order for 50 Martin 303s, a pressurized version of the 202, with which Martin was not in a position to proceed when the 202 was found to have a design flaw that caused catastrophic wing failure. By the time the 202 was transformed into the 404 for Eastern and TWA, United had chosen the Convair 340. This airplane was a stretched version of the CV 240 so successfully launched by American, and had improved hot- and high-altitude performance, a useful asset on United's routes over the Rockies. Commencing in March 1952, the fleet of CV 340s, which numbered 52 at its high point, served United for 16 years without a fatal accident.

By the early 1950s, United placed its last big piston propliner orders. The DC-6 fleet grew with the addition of the slightly larger DC-6B, the most productive piston liner ever made. Equipped with higher-powered engines and benefiting from an increase in fuel load and maximum gross weight, it effectively neutralized the Constellation 649s and 749s and maintained a slight edge in speed over them. Forty-three DC-6Bs flew in United colors starting in

The DC-6 was Douglas' first pressurized airliner. It competed against the Lockheed L-049 Constellation and outperformed it, setting off a decade-long duel between the two companies that led to the ultimate piston liners. The last DC-6B retired from the United fleet in 1970.

United passed on the turboprops, preferring to go straight to jets, but ended up with a fleet of Vickers Viscounts when it acquired Capital Airlines in 1961. The acquisition made it America's biggest airline ahead of rival American, and it found an excellent niche role for the Viscounts on routes shorter than 200 miles, which they served for a decade.

1951. The last one was delivered in 1958, and the last to retire flew the line until 1970.

In mid-1952, the company signed an order for 25 DC-7s to compete with TWA's Constellations and American's own DC-7s. For the first time, when DC-7s started flying, an airline in scheduled service was able to cross the U.S. continent nonstop, west to east, in a little over eight hours. It took some time to establish regular nonstop service industrywide because of a labor dispute about marginally exceeding the eight-hour limit on pilot flight time on the crossings.

United received the first of its DC-7s in early 1954. They usurped the DC-6Bs in transcontinental and Hawaiian service, initially in first class configuration followed by coach as demand for inexpensive travel soared. The initial order was followed up, and a total of 58 DC-7s were accepted by United through 1958. Although well received by passengers for their comfort, speed, and range, they were marginally economical because of the excessive unscheduled maintenance required by their turbo-compound engines.

As the CAB rationed out competition in increasing doses during the late 1940s and the 1950s, the scramble for passengers intensified. United was

In the 1950s, concern about safety was still an active issue among air travelers and the airlines allayed their fears in part with the publicizing of how things worked. This 1953 description of the instrument landing system is a notably clear and reassuring explanation.

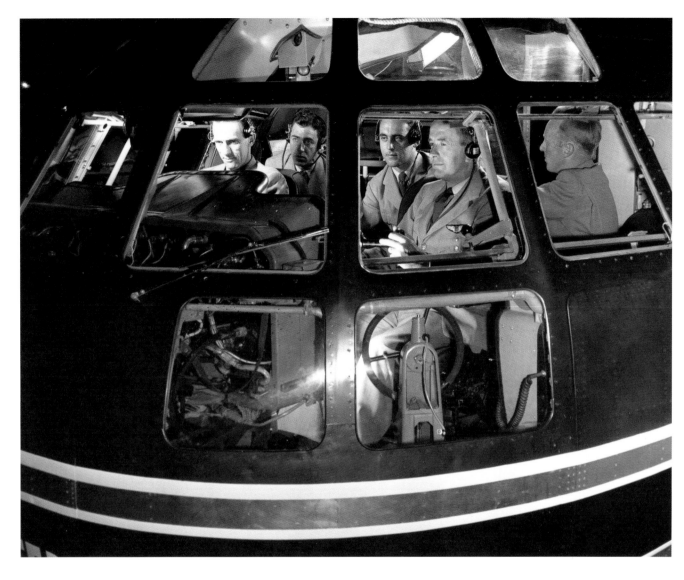

The Stratocruiser's greenhouse cockpit was packed with crew members. Today it only takes two pilots to fly an airliner, the rest have been replaced by technology.

quick to coddle its customers to win their loyalty. The family fare plan, adopted industrywide, that allowed family members to accompany the ticketholder at half price during midweek was highly successful. DC-7 Red Carpet flights featured aircraft with custom pastel interiors, plush leather cabin accents, exceptional cabin service, and a red carpet at the door.

United even came up with a service that seems downright odious today but was all the rage in its time and lasted into the early jet age. It was a men-only daily executive flight on the Chicago–New York and San Francisco–Los Angeles routes, complete with free-flowing liquor, steak dinners, cigars on the house, and slippers for the boys.

Patterson did have a strong personal distaste for serving alcohol on airliners. After holding out for many years, he had given in reluctantly for competitive reasons. However, he limited liquor service to

two drinks per passenger on each flight, and in 1956 he succeeded in convincing five other trunk carriers to adopt the same policy.

Another point of intense competition was the postwar introduction of cut-rate air coach fares in 1948. Although United had pioneered the concept in 1940 on the San Francisco–Los Angeles run, it was reluctant to embrace coach class, fearing an erosion of profit margins. But by 1950 competition forced it to join the crowd, setting off an absurd tangle over it with the CAB bureaucracy. Reluctant to squeeze coach passengers into the cabin like sardines, United provided more generous legroom than the industry standard, only to be told by the CAB that it was competing unfairly and must cram more coach seats aboard.

In spite of some misgivings, air coach was a big hit, accounting for more than a third of United's mainland flights and more than half of Hawaiian

Passengers arriving in Hawaii were often accorded a lavish traditional greeting and leis were obligatory. The airlines made Hawaii available to a wider clientele and turned it from an exclusive retreat for the wealthy into a popular destination for the emerging middle class.

flights by 1956. TWA introduced mixed first class and coach service in the United States in 1955, and United followed suit about a year later.

Airline safety was also steadily improving during this time, and United made particularly important contributions to the development of a practical airborne weather radar. The effort was led by communications director Russ Cunningham, who had iced up and crash-landed in his Boeing B-40 mail plane in Oregon in the late 1920s as he experimented with homing in on radio signals. Between 1955 and 1957, United's fleet became the first to be fully radar equipped.

A few months after their introduction, two United DC-7s dramatically demonstrated how much the world had shrunk by 1954. They took off from New York at sunrise and headed west, reaching Hawaii by sunset after 17 hours in the air and one refueling stop. They arrived in time for their VIP passengers to comfortably make a gala dinner at the Royal Hawaiian on Waikiki Beach. But the time was not far off when the DC-7s, propellerless successors on the same flight would get their charges to Honolulu in time for lunch.

United planned meticulously for the jet age. As early as 1952 its Jetliner Committee conducted an intriguing experiment, the Paper Jet project. The object of the exercise was to determine whether jet airliners could successfully fit into the much slower traffic flow of the propeller liners. Over a period of several days, jet flights were simulated in real time between San Francisco and New York taking into consideration the weather and the day's real traffic. The conclusion was that the jets would do just fine, and the search for United's first jet gathered momentum. Given the preponderance of long-haul

routes in its system, United decided to forego the interim turboprop stage and opted to transition directly to pure jets.

Following discussions with Boeing, which already had the Dash 80 prototype flying, and Douglas, which was still in the early design stage of the DC-8, United chose the DC-8 with an order for 30 of the jetliners on October 25, 1955. The main reason for remaining loyal to Douglas was the possibility of incorporating design changes sought by the airline.

United particularly wanted a wider fuselage to allow six-abreast seating. Boeing, having built the tooling for the 707, categorically ruled out such a change but Douglas was able to readily agree because the DC-8 was still only on the drawing board. The drawback of opting for the DC-8 was a one-year wait in introducing jet service behind the airlines that chose the Boeing 707. This delay, however, was not seen as big a disadvantage at the time as it seems today, because many airline executives

believed that the public's acceptance of jet travel would be a gradual process. Interestingly enough, a few days after United signed the DC-8 contract Boeing gave in to its own customers' demands to widen the Dash 80 fuselage.

In 1957 United increased its DC-8 order to 40 aircraft, but Boeing didn't entirely lose the airline in the early jet game. Like many of its competitors, United needed a shorter-range jet for its medium routes and Boeing had developed one by scaling down the 707. It was the Boeing 720, 18 feet shorter, some 50,000 pounds lighter, and with improved hot and high performance. In late 1957 United ordered 11 of them (later increased to 29) for first deliveries in 1960.

When American Airlines introduced transcontinental jet service in September 1958 followed closely by TWA, the public's acceptance was so overwhelming that United had to abandon nonstop transcontinental DC-7 service. Many travelers chose to be put on standby if a jet flight was fully booked and would

When United's plans to acquire a pressurized version of the Martin 202 fell through because of wing structural problems with the original 202, the airline selected the Convair 340 as its DC-3 replacement. As many as 52 CV 340s served United for 16 years without a fatal accident.

The DC-7 ad claiming a 7.5-hour transcontinental crossing isn't concerned with truth in advertising. The real life average was just beyond eight hours, especially on westbound trips, and caused a row with the Airline Pilots' Association about crew duty times.

grudgingly shuffle on the propliners only if the jets left them behind.

Reprieve came on September 18, 1959 when two of the long-awaited DC-8s simultaneously inaugurated United jet service in both directions between San Francisco and New York. The passengers came flocking back to the fold, and the jets were soon whisking them all the way to Hawaii. To regain some lost momentum, United's DC-8s set a string of speed records. Most impressive among them was a 7 hour 52 minute nonstop flight from Honolulu to Chicago. It was a VIP flight with Pat Patterson on board. The DC-8 was named *Annie Johnson* in honor of the schooner, which, 47 years before, had taken three weeks to bring a 13-year-old Patterson from Honolulu to San Francisco to seek his fortune.

When it introduced the DC-8, United also put on a unique year-long road show called "Jetarama" to popularize jet travel among infrequent fliers. Three circus tents were set up on the tarmac of a major airport, framing a United jet parked before them. Visitors were treated to a comprehensive exhibit explaining the workings and possibilities of the jet age followed by a tour of the jetliner. Among the more interesting exhibits was a preview of United's Instamatic computer reservation system then being installed, which rivaled American's pioneering Sabre system and was succeeded in 1972 by Apollo.

Another United contribution to the jet age was the telescopic terminal jetway that put an end to having to brave the elements to board an airplane.

In 1960 United put in service its first Boeing 720s to popular acclaim, especially on high-density medium-haul routes such as the Chicago–New York run. But the company still needed a shorter-haul jet, and because U.S. manufacturers were slow to oblige, it looked abroad for a solution and found it in the capable and aesthetically beautiful, twin-engined, French Caravelle.

The company ordered 20 "La Belle Caravelles" for delivery the next year. They served ably for a decade before being replaced primarily by Boeing 737s. They also added a touch of French flair to those men-only executive flights between Chicago and New York, and claimed another historic first for the airline. In December 1964, a United Caravelle was the first airliner operated by a U.S. airline to make an autopilot-controlled fully automatic landing in scheduled service, monitored by the pilots with their hands in their lap.

In 1961 United regained a distinction it had lost in 1937. It once again became America's biggest air-line. It reclaimed the top spot from American by acquiring Capital Airlines, a scrappy Washington, D.C.-based East Coast regional that had overreached its ability to expand and ran into financial difficulties. With the Capital acquisition, United added a readymade East Coast network that it had coveted since the 1930s.

Capital traced its roots all the way back to 1927 and the Clifford Ball Airline that flew the mail between Pittsburgh and Cleveland. Through a series of mergers, Clifford Ball absorbed Kohler Aviation, gaining routes as far as Detroit and Milwaukee, and became Pennsylvania Central Airlines, operating a fleet of DC-3s. It was renamed Capital Airlines after World War II and rapidly expanded southward along the eastern seaboard, encouraged by the CAB out to chip away at Eastern's near-monopoly.

Capital rapidly built up a fleet of DC-4s, DC-6s, DC-7s, and Lockheed Constellations, and like other feisty regionals, it even claimed a couple of firsts. In 1948 it was the first U.S. airline to start sustained

The Douglas DC-8 was co-launched by United with Delta on September 18, 1959. United's inaugural event was the simultaneous departure in opposite directions of two DC-8s between San Francisco and New York. United also put on a yearlong road show called Jetarama to popularize jet travel. Presented at airports nationwide, Jetarama's top attraction was a tour of a United jet.

The DC-8's galley was a long way from the DC-3's thermos bottles full of creamed chicken. Custom-designed food trays and serving dishes were an important part of attempting to distinguish an airline from its competitors.

coach service. It was a move motivated by competition from the nonscheduled operators and was quickly adopted by the rest of the scheduled airlines.

Less known is that Capital was the first U.S. airline to operate a turbine airliner, the 400-miles per hour, four-engined, 48-seat British Vickers Viscount. Capital introduced the plane in July 1955 with excellent results, but made one error that was to prove its undoing. It bought far too many of them, mostly on debt. The cash flow wasn't there to service Capital's financial commitments, and as soon as the higher-capacity turboprop Electra and the jets made their appearance on the routes served by the Viscounts, the airline was doomed.

United, which made a conscious decision to bypass the turboprops now found itself with a large fleet of Viscounts, and it ended up keeping 47 of them. The Viscounts proved to be a good money-maker on routes not longer than 200 miles and roamed the eastern U.S. skies in United colors for almost a decade after the merger.

In the 1960s United made four major jet decisions, playing a launch role in two of them. It was the co-launch customer for the Boeing 727; it was the U.S. launch customer of the Boeing 737; and it entered the widebody era with the obligatory purchase of Boeing 747s and a substantial order for the Douglas DC-10.

United ordered its first batch of Boeing 727s in 1960, the same year it bought the Caravelles. The airline played a key role with Eastern in helping Boeing develop the 727 to meet the need for an airliner that could use 5,000-feet runways and make money on trip lengths ranging from 150 miles to 2,000 miles. The airplane's triple-slotted Fowler flaps, which increase the wing area by 25 percent were the technical breakthrough that enabled it to meet the requisite runway performance.

The 727 was United's first self-sufficient jet, equipped with its own APU and a rear airstair door, freeing it from the need for any ground equipment. The first United 727, delivered in late 1963 and put in service in April 1964, can still be seen today at Seattle's Museum of Flight.

Amusing the youngest passengers has always been a challenge for the airlines. Kids traveling first class in the 1950s and early 1960s were given a veritable toy store of goodies by some airlines to keep them busy.

The 737 was Boeing's answer to the Douglas DC-9, and the company succeeded in convincing United to break with its Douglas tradition to buy it. The launch customer for the type was the German airline, Lufthansa, the first foreign carrier to launch a U.S. airliner. United's order for 40 737s in April 1965 was only two months behind Lufthansa's and was for the stretched 200 series, which accommodated 130 coach class passengers compared to 100 on Lufthansa's initial aircraft.

The Boeing 737 order was the centerpiece of Pat Patterson's last act before he retired. In 1965 he electrified the airline industry by committing United to purchasing 112 new aircraft for a staggering $750 million. The breakdown was 40 737s with an option for 30 more, 20 727s; 15 727QCs, quick conversion models for passenger or cargo use; and 7 DC-8-61s.

The 200-passenger stretched Super DC-8-61s were a precursor to the coming widebody era to handle a perceived need for substantially higher passenger

United and other U.S. airlines wanted a short-haul jet but American manufacturers were slow in producing them, so the airlines turned overseas. United opted for the French Sud Aviation Caravelle, ordering 20 of the graceful twinjets. They entered service in 1961 and flew for United for a decade. In 1964 a United Caravelle became the first airliner flying with a U.S. airline to make a fully automatic autopilot-controlled landing on a scheduled flight.

loads per flight. What most of the domestic U.S. airlines really needed was a 250–300 passenger widebody, but Juan Trippe had sprung the 350–400 seat Boeing 747 on the world and all but one of the U.S. trunk carriers felt compelled to have it.

United's original 747 fleet consisted of 18 aircraft, delivered between 1970 and 1973. They were introduced on the prestigious New York–San Francisco–Hawaii run and were largely employed on Hawaiian services. Since the mid-1960s, hopes had

United acquired 18 Boeing 747s, delivered between 1970 and 1973. The smaller DC-10s were more suited for most of United's routes but the 747s served on transcontinental runs and especially the Hawaii route. After deregulation, when United became a major international carrier, it acquired additional 747s for its transoceanic routes.

This photo of the Boeing 727's air stair illustrates the airplane's self-sufficiency. With its onboard auxiliary power unit, it was the first airliner of its size that could operate out of an airport without any need for ground support.

been high that United would receive authorization to fly to the Far East, where the 747s would have been ideal, but a 1969 CAB decision turned down all of United's applications, much to United's great disappointment. Nevertheless, unlike several other domestic carriers, which soon concluded that the original jumbo jet was too large for their routes, United continued to operate its original 747s well into the era of deregulation, when they were joined by additional 747s as United expanded internationally.

Smaller widebodies were not far behind the 747, and although United selected the DC-10 several months after American Airlines, its order for 30 aircraft with an option on an additional 30 was significantly larger. It reinforced Douglas' commitment to the program at a time when the manufacturer was suffering severe cash flow problems due to mismanagement that caused the slippage of deliveries on a healthy order book. The McDonnell Corporation's acquisition of Douglas and a concurrent massive

United was the first U.S. customer for the Boeing 737, ordering 40 of them two months behind Lufthansa, the first foreign launch customer for a U.S. airliner. The 737 was the short-haul jet United had been waiting for since the early 1960s. In various more recent models, it continues to be one of the most prominent aircraft in United's fleet.

cash infusion in turn gave the airlines confidence in Douglas' ability to perform.

United inaugurated DC-10 service in August 1971 from San Francisco to Washington Dulles. Ultimately 48 DC-10s were acquired by United from its original order, all Dash 10s. In spite of the type's well-publicized early problems, they proved to be a real workhorse on the company's high-density coast-to-coast and medium-haul routes. The last ones flew with United into the twenty-first century.

By the time the DC-10 entered service, United was experiencing financial losses due to a fall off in traffic caused by excess capacity, an excessive debt load, and the beginnings of a long, agonizing period of national economic decline soon to be exacerbated by the 1973 oil crisis. The airline continued to experience a challenging time into the early 1980s as it attempted to diversify into nonaviation businesses, went through a succession of chief executives, and was acquired by an investor group that refocused it on its core business.

But it never lost its preeminent position and ultimately, in an innovative and unusual move, several of its employee groups became its majority owners, acquiring a 55 percent share of the company and shielding it from the threat of Lorenzo-style takeovers. Deregulation has been good for United, giving it the international routes it had sought in vain from the CAB. It acquired Pan American's Pacific Division and its London routes and built upon them to form its own global network. And in 1984, it became the first airline to serve all of America's 50 states.

CHAPTER 4

Eastern

Captain Eddie Rickenbacker, Eastern Airlines' feisty, hawk-faced president was reviewing interior options for the luxurious Lockheed Constellations his airline had recently ordered. He was shown the opulent leather upholstery a competitor had chosen. "What would you like to see on those 88 seats on Eastern's planes, Captain Rickenbacker?" asked the company representative. "Eighty-eight asses!" snapped the old fighter pilot.

For Captain Eddie and his airline, it always was about the bottom line. The first of the Big Four to go off government subsidy, Eastern had a reputation for being a no-nonsense, tight-fisted airline more concerned with profitably getting its passengers to their destinations than coddling them on the lap of luxury.

Like all reputations, it was only half true. Rickenbacker never scrimped on equipment, was fanatical about safety, and highly respected his pilots' judgment, yet he refused to install autopilots for years, because he dismissed them as expensive, unreliable gadgetry. Eastern was the only airline that prompted the formation of a hate club by malcontent passengers, yet it invented one of the most innovative and lucrative airline services, the Eastern Shuttle. And in the context of history, intervals of serious lapses in looking after its passengers excessively overshadowed long periods of general customer satisfaction.

Eastern evolved from Pitcairn Aviation, one of the most efficient air mail carriers of the late 1920s with a route stretching all the way from New York to Miami via Atlanta, and connecting with Pan American's network to points further south. Pitcairn was created by talented aircraft designer Harold Pitcairn, whose 16 graceful Mailwing biplanes of his own design plied the mail route with unprecedented reliability.

But Pitcairn's heart was in aircraft design, so in July 1929 he sold the mail line to an eager Clement Keys whose North American Aviation conglomerate was one of the biggest players in the aviation industry. It already controlled two important airlines, NAT, which would later be absorbed by United; and Transcontinental Air Transport, which would become part of TWA; and also counted Sperry Gyroscope and Curtiss Aircraft among its holdings.

The mail flights continued, but Keys had acquired Pitcairn with passenger service in mind. He ordered three Ford Trimotors and renamed the company Eastern Air Transport just in time for the Watres-McNary Act of 1930 and the spoils conferences that followed. Having lost control of NAT to United Aircraft in a corporate struggle, Keys' other airline interests emerged in good shape when the dust settled. Transcontinental Air Transport was now Transcontinental and Western Airlines holding the central transcontinental route, and Eastern Air

The Ford Trimotor Tin Goose was one of Eastern's first aircraft. It was ordered by Pitcairn in 1929 before he sold the airline to Clement Keys whose North American Aviation conglomerate also controlled Transcontinental Air Transport, National Air Transport, Curtiss Aircraft, and Sperry Gyroscope. Keys renamed Pitcairn Aviation, Eastern Air Transport. This aircraft is flown by the Experimental Aircraft Association out of Oshkosh, Wisconsin, and at times offers rides to let modern-day travelers experience air travel in the late 1920s. *Lawrence Feir*

In December 1930 Eastern placed the first Curtiss Condor in service between New York and Atlanta. Eastern was a natural launch customer for the Curtiss Condor, because Curtiss was a sister company. This later model Condor (the first ones had double vertical stabilizers) is the most luxurious aircraft of its time and the first to offer sleeper service, initially on American Airlines. But it was under-powered and slow and was soon eclipsed by the more modern Douglas all-metal airliners.

Transport was the north-south trunk line in the eastern United States.

On August 18, 1930, Eastern inaugurated its first passenger service, flying from New York to Richmond, Virginia, via Newark, Philadelphia, Baltimore, and Washington. In short order, the company also placed a big order for new equipment that included six stately Curtiss Condors with which Keys was hoping to corner the airliner market.

The Condors were under development and keenly anticipated long before Eastern formally ordered them from its sister company. The first Condors went into service in December 1930 between New York and Atlanta and by early 1931, Eastern was carrying passengers all the way down to Miami. Though woefully under-powered, the Condors were the height of airborne luxury compared to the Fords and Fokkers, and quickly found favor with their passengers. With the Condors came Eastern's first stewardesses.

Among them was Mildred Aldrin, whose nephew, Buzz, would stroll on the moon.

In 1931 Eastern was one of the first airlines to require an instrument rating from its pilots and equip its airplanes with radios capable of voice communication. This move marked the beginning of a well-deserved reputation Eastern acquired over the years for being an exceptionally experienced bad weather airline.

Eastern established its northern operations center in Newark, which was maturing into New York's main airport, and was progressing nicely when in late 1931, Keys' business empire collapsed. Several of his partners had surreptitiously speculated on the stock market with North American's funds and had bet the wrong way. In exchange for bailing out Keys, a consortium of banks took control of North American and its operating companies.

With its reliable performance and long route network, Eastern became an attractive target for United Aircraft, which indirectly bought up enough shares in Eastern to seize control. Postmaster General Brown, however, would have none of it. A big point of the spoils conferences, after all, was to give United competition. He forced United to sell its shares. And therein Captain Edward V. Rickenbacker, World War I flying ace and former General Motors (GM) and American Airlines executive, saw an opportunity. He convinced GM to acquire control of North American Aviation and install him to look after Eastern Air Transport.

But by the time GM gained control on February 28, 1933, a Democrat was sitting in the White House, and was considerably more suspicious of big business than his Republican predecessor. Franklin D. Roosevelt was receptive to accusations of bid fixing by a Senate investigation triggered by revelations that Eastern had won an air mail route with a higher bid than the

Eastern's falcon logo was adopted in 1935. The background is the sun, partially eclipsed by the falcon's wing. It remained Eastern's motif until the 1960s. In time the falcon also found its place on the tail of Eastern's airliners.

A Eastern Stinson Reliant VIP aircraft publicizing the 1939 New York World's Fair. Miss World's Fair is flanked by an Eastern captain (note that captains rated only two stripes in the early days) and an Eastern steward. Eastern's president, Captain Eddie Rickenbacker replaced stewardesses with stewards in 1936 to save on training costs. Stewardesses were not allowed to be married so many had to resign after only a few years of service when they decided to tie the knot, and replacements had to be trained.

Ludington Line. In early 1934, he cancelled all air mail contracts with the airlines and transferred the task to the Army Air Corps.

The captain wasn't amused. When three hapless air mail pilots crashed and died in one day just trying to get to their air mail bases to begin carrying the mail, Rickenbacker publicly accused the Roosevelt administration of legalized murder. Then he helped the airline industry make a point. He hopped on board the prototype DC-1 with Jack Frye, president of TWA, and the pair set a record from Los Angeles to New York, arriving through a blizzard after only 13 hours and 4 minutes.

More Army fliers died needlessly. Within a month the airlines were asked to rebid on their air mail contracts under the 1934 Air Mail Act with some cosmetic measures attached. One required that the routes not be given back to the airlines that had held them. They all got around it by simply changing their name. Eastern Air Transport became Eastern Airlines and Captain Eddie was named its president.

Hot on the heels of the re-awarded routes came the introduction of Eastern's first DC-2 of the nine on order. Piloted personally by Rickenbacker, it launched DC-2 *Florida Flyer* service from New York to Miami in 10 hours, three less than the Condors. The big ungainly Condors were all gone by the end of 1935, including the newer sleeper versions instigated by American Airlines, a few of which Eastern had also purchased. Five speedy, modern Lockheed 10 Electras joined Eastern's growing DC-2 fleet to work the feeder routes.

Eastern was also expanding its domain. It successfully bid for the crucial Chicago-Atlanta route that tapped into the important midwestern market, and also secured access to New Orleans. To handle the extra traffic, five more DC-2s joined the fleet. The company relocated its main operations center from Atlanta to Miami, and in 1935, the first full year of Rickenbacker's reign, it turned a profit for the first time. It would rack up an unbroken profitability record for the next 26 years.

At about this time Eastern became aware of a small thorn in its side, called National Airlines. Even though the adjective "national" hardly fit the tiny Tampa, Florida-based carrier, it went after Eastern's local expansion plans in bulldog fashion. Over time the feud would become an industry legend.

In 1936, as a prime example of Rickenbacker's bottom line-focused management style,

The Great Silver Fleet was a name dreamed up in the mid-1930s by Captain Rickenbacker who was inspired by the bare metal finish of the new modern airliners being delivered to the company. It alternatively appeared across the fuselage with the term *Eastern Airlines*. This item is a souvenir map sponsored by Gulf Oil Company, aviation gas suppliers to Eastern.

he phased out all the stewardesses and replaced them with male stewards. It was purely a matter of economics. Stewardesses, who had to be single by industry policy in those days, rarely stayed more than a year or two before they quit to get married and a replacement had to be trained. Rickenbacker rightly reasoned that male stewards would stay longer, dramatically cutting training costs for the airline.

Eastern's shiny Douglas airliners were dressed in a lively fresh livery featuring the company's new falcon logo and were collectively christened the Great Silver Fleet. Coincidentally Eastern took delivery of its first two DC-3s, with eight more to come on line in quick succession.

In 1937, Eastern's deep commitment to high technical standards was recognized when the National Safety Council presented it with a special

award in recognition of flying for seven years without a single fatality.

The following year brought important developments. Eddie Rickenbacker lined up financial support with the help of Kuhn Loeb and Company and on April 22, 1938, he bought Eastern Airlines from General Motors. The auto giant never really saw itself as a committed airline operator and decided to shed its modestly profitable investment. Rickenbacker and his backers outbid John Hertz, Yellow Cab tycoon and future rental car magnate, no small feat on Wall Street's mean streets.

Eastern settled comfortably into its role as one of the Big Four with its ever growing DC-3 fleet, and even managed to scoop American on the opening of Washington National airport in 1941. The first landing was promised to American Airlines, and C. R. Smith's public relations staff was turning it into a major media event. But the American flight was slightly late, and meanwhile an Eastern DC-3 scheduled to arrive behind it sailed into National's airspace. The controllers tried to make it wait, but Eastern raised such hell about its right to arrive on schedule that they let it swoop down to land before the row of photographers expecting the arrival of American.

Such turf wars were soon trivialized by the horrors of World War II, and the Great Silver Fleet was joined by the Great Chocolate Fleet. Eastern formed a separate Military Transport Division to make its contribution to Air Transport Command (ATC) and flew primarily Curtiss C-46 Commandos painted chocolate brown. As the war progressed, the company's main route was from Miami to Accra, Ghana, in West Africa along the South Atlantic route to Asia. Eastern's stewards had marched off to war, so Captain Eddie had to relent and hire stewardesses once again for the fleet that remained in civilian service after 20 of its DC-3s were drafted by the Army.

Eastern's bad weather experience was put to unusual use as the ATC airlift got under way. Its training pilots were assigned to give instrument refresher training to some of Pan American's crews who had little instrument flying experience along the balmy fair weather routes to which they had been assigned before the war.

Eastern's Great Chocolate Fleet lost only one airplane during the entire war, but the airline almost lost Eddie Rickenbacker. The captain was on an inspection tour on behalf of the government, flying as a passenger on an Army B-17 crossing the Pacific when it got lost on the way to Canton Island. They missed the drop in the ocean that they were aiming for 1,800 miles from Honolulu on the way to Australia

Eastern's DC-4s were actually surplus C-54 Skymasters converted to civilian use and leased from the military. Eastern flew a total of 32 Skymasters between 1946 and 1955.

and had to ditch when they ran out of fuel. Rickenbacker and his companions spent 22 epic days in life rafts with no food and minimal water before being rescued 500 miles from their original destination. All but one survived the ordeal.

Captain Eddie resumed his inspection tour as soon as he felt sufficiently rehydrated, but as the war was drawing to a close, he was already preparing for its aftermath. In 1944, Eastern ordered 14 Lockheed Constellations, third in line for the type behind TWA and Pan American. An advantage of being a late-comer was getting the more advanced 649 model instead of the earlier 049.

By 1946, Eastern had gotten back all of its DC-3s plus a few new ones and was also flying 19 DC-4s at last. It had been awarded new routes from New York to St. Louis, and, more significantly, to Boston, and the Constellations were on their way. The only speck of cloud on Eastern's horizon was increasing competition from Delta and National.

George Baker's small, aggressive Buccaneer line especially ruffled Eastern's feathers. Thanks to the CAB's postwar maneuvering to increase competition among the airlines, National was awarded rights to service between New York and Miami, Eastern's jewel in the crown, and it moved quickly to scoop its big rival. Rushing into service its first DC-4s, a big

step up from the Lockheed Lodestar, National beat Eastern to nonstop New York–Miami service.

When the Constellations finally did enter service, they quickly reclaimed Eastern's preeminent position for the time being. Being put under pressure by National's emphasis on luxury, Eastern fought back with a dependability theme.

Eastern's next equipment decision after choosing the Constellations was finding a replacement for the venerable DC-3. The company cautiously flirted with the Martin 202, finding the alternative airplane, the Convair 240, faster on takeoffs and landings and therefore needing more runway. But Eastern insisted on being able to make design changes to the 202 before making a commitment, which Martin was unwilling to accept. Eastern put off the decision and saved itself from a major fiasco when the fatal structural weakness of the 202's wing was catastrophically revealed in a Northwest accident.

One consequence of the Northwest tragedy was that Eastern got its chance to redesign the Martin 202. The airplane that emerged was the Martin 404, equipped with a completely redesigned wing joint and a pressurized cabin among many other changes. Eastern signed up for a total of 60 Martin 404s. The first one went into service in 1950 and the 404 fleet roamed the short-haul routes for a decade

Captain Eddie Rickenbacker checking out a new Eastern Constellation at Lockheed in Burbank, California. Rickenbacker was fanatical about safety and efficiency but not particularly moved by luxury and marketing, an attitude reflected by the airline in the minds of many passengers.

without a single fatal accident before being replaced by turbine equipment.

Eastern's business soared in the 1950s as Florida grew exponentially into a prime vacation and retirement destination. But the airline wasn't just benefiting from the Sunshine State's economic boom. It helped create it along with its rivals, National and Delta. Florida hotels stayed open during the summer for the first time in 1949 largely on the strength of the airlines' promise to funnel off-season vacationers their way. As the nation's economy prospered, the middle classes' attention turned increasingly to leisure activities, and they had the money to spare for airline tickets to whisk them off on their getaways.

And in the middle of the decade, Eastern gave their mobility a major boost. It converted half of its capacity to coach class. Airlines had been offering coach on a large scale since 1948, but the level of Eastern's new commitment was unprecedented. The era of mass air travel was beginning to gather steam.

The future looked rosy and Eddie Rickenbacker went on a shopping spree. In 1952, he ordered 30 L-1049C Super C Constellations. In 1955, he announced that the Constellations would become an all-coach fleet and signed up for 40 DC-7s, the first Eastern Douglas aircraft to feature ovens instead of the food thermos jugs. And then he committed Eastern to the turbine age. First he placed an order for 40 Lockheed L-188 Electra turboprops with options on another 30. Then he signed for 16 Douglas DC-8s and options for 8 more.

Rickenbacker placed such big orders based on Eastern's perceptions of potential traffic growth and his view of the coming jet age. Traffic growth expectations turned out to be too optimistic not only because total traffic increases in Eastern's territory fell short of the mark, but because Eastern had a difficult time convincing the CAB to award it additional routes. Fierce competition from National and Delta and negligible route expansion led to overcapacity.

Compounding the problem was Eastern's chosen transition path to jets. The ever cautious Rickenbacker was convinced that the turboprops would have a reasonably long interim role before the switch to pure jets, hence his aggressive order for the Electras. Complicating his decision was the relative incompatibility with most of Eastern's route structure of the two available choices, the DC-8 and the B-707, both designed for long-haul flights.

Eastern did beat both Delta and National to ordering the DC-8, but then Rickenbacker made a controversial decision that gave away his airline's lead.

Learning that the DC-8 would soon be available with the more powerful JT-4 engine that eliminated the need for water injection to boost power on takeoff, he gave up Eastern's first six DC-8 positions to wait for the later model. The airline that snapped them up was Delta.

Delta's DC-8s beat Eastern into service by a year when they started flying between New York and Houston. They were an instant success with passengers, siphoning them off Eastern's competing Electras in unprecedented numbers.

And the irascible George Baker upstaged not only Eastern but also the entire domestic industry with a typically innovative move. The Buccaneer line moved swiftly to lease two Pan American Boeing 707s for the 1958 winter season (when Pan Am's traffic on its European routes was comparatively low) and ran them between New York and Miami, to become the first domestic U.S. airline to start jet service.

The consequences of Eastern's equipment decisions and stiffening competition set the stage for a period of financial difficulties and decline in service. Passengers came to so dislike Eastern that when a pair of frustrated Philadelphia businessmen formed a tongue-in-cheek We Hate Eastern Airlines (WHEAL) club, they got hundreds of members who were totally serious.

The company was groaning under a huge debt burden financing an obsolete, underutilized fleet. It was a tough challenge to meet, and Eastern's board decided that it was time for Eddie Rickenbacker to hand over the reins. He was eased up to chairman as a succession of new senior executives grappled with Eastern's problems over the next decade.

In 1960, Eastern suffered its first loss in 26 years. In the next five years its cumulative net loss would total $70 million. Energetic steps were taken to stem the flood of red ink, but the size of the problem precluded quick solutions. Immediate steps were taken to purchase 15 Boeing 720s between 1961 and 1963 as an interim solution to the shortage of DC-8s, and a real effort was mounted to upgrade service to win back customers. And as the launch customer for Boeing's new three-engined medium-haul design, the Boeing 727, Eastern was heavily involved in developing the jet that was to become Boeing's best seller. It ordered 40 of them with options for another 10.

In improving its image, Eastern took a cue from one of the classiest airlines of the time by hiring TWA's head of operations, Floyd Hall, as its president and CEO in 1963. Hall faced a heavily indebted airline with a jet fleet that amounted to only 50 percent of its total fleet and was in dire need of short-haul

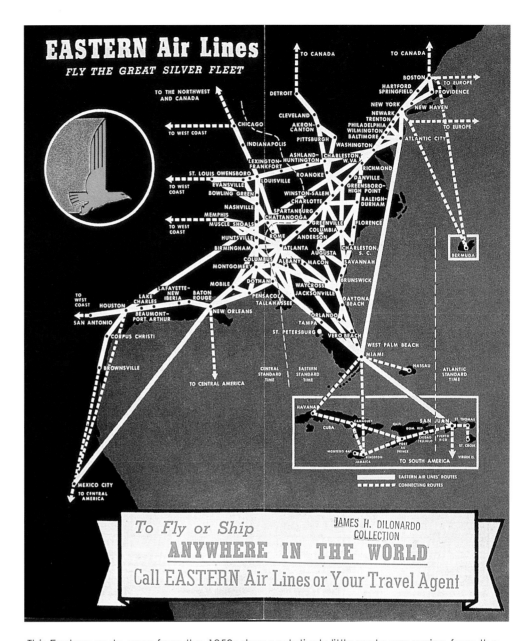

This Eastern route map from the 1950s shows relatively little route expansion from the 1930s. Important additions were routes to New England, Puerto Rico, Mexico, and a direct route between New York and Miami. But Eastern had no monopoly on any of them, and coveted routes to the Southwest were not forthcoming. The company felt constrained by the lack of new route awards as the CAB ratcheted up competition by favoring the growth of National and Delta.

Golden Falcon

EASTERN AIR LINES

Eastern's Golden Falcon service was up against Delta's Royal Crown flights, which featured an extra stewardess and somewhat more lavish amenities. Eastern's response to the luxury challenge was the dependability theme and the convenience of more frequent service.

equipment. He cajoled an order of DC-9s out of Douglas and mounted an intense marketing campaign.

Eastern's art deco falcon logo was superceded by an elegantly simple stylized falcon, and the blue and burnt orange colors were exchanged for two shades of blue. New uniforms were introduced, and staff was trained to serve with a smile. Battles were fought with Eastern's old guard about the quality of the china to be used on board, and the food served on it was markedly improved. The VIP Falcon Lounges became Ionosphere Rooms, and Eastern was presented as the Wings of Man. Passenger satisfaction soared, the WHEAL club was officially disbanded, and in 1965 Eastern was again profitable—for the moment.

Eastern's biggest coup to bolster its share of the lucrative Florida market in the mid-1960s was landing an agreement to become the official carrier of Disney World, Disney's wildly successful East Coast venture destined for Orlando.

Another boost to the bottom line came from Eastern's most innovative contribution to air transportation, the Eastern Shuttle. Other airlines had experimented briefly with the concept, but Eastern was the one that made it work. Linking New York and

Boston and New York and Washington, it worked on the principle of simple, fast, and above all, guaranteed service. It guaranteed seating to all comers without any need for reservations or tickets purchased in advance. Passengers just showed up, boarded the airplane, and paid for their tickets in flight.

The shuttle worked because it had a dedicated fleet with each scheduled departure backed up by a reserve aircraft to take any overflow. But when it was launched in 1961 with a fleet of Constellations backed up by Martin 404s, it was an uncertain experiment. Nobody knew whether it would be profitable. With practice, however, the traffic flows became predictable and the shuttle turned into one of the airline's biggest money-makers. It also provided an opportunity to make profitable use of Eastern's Electras, which gradually replaced the aging Constellations in shuttle service and served valiantly until 1978 when they were replaced by the jets.

Bolstered by the shuttle's success, Eastern tried the concept between New York and Miami in 1963 with dismal results. The long-haul route with its seasonal swings simply wasn't suited for the service. Passenger demand wasn't even in both directions, resulting in a lot of empty seats on one of the segments depending

on the time of year. The guaranteed seating feature also posed problems. It was excessively costly to fly a half-empty backup aircraft the entire length of the East Coast (compared to the short hop from New York to Boston or Washington), and the experiment was quickly abandoned.

The introduction of the 727 was a much greater success. Here was the profitable medium-haul workhorse of a jet that Eastern so badly craved. The airplane was tailor-made for the company's route system. Its three fan-jet engines cured the shortage of power suffered by the first generation of jetliners. But the most innovative feature that made it capable of operating in and out of the short local and regional fields dotting Eastern's network was its wings.

In cruise configuration, they sliced through the air to enable the airplane to efficiently achieve a high cruise speed. For landing, however, (and to a lesser extent for takeoff) their shape was completely transformed by leading edge slats and triple-slotted trailing edge flaps into a high lift structure that could sustain lift at low speeds, giving it excellent

short-field performance. As one captain famously remarked, "You don't lower the flaps on this airplane—you take apart the whole damned wing." The 727-100 series was in short order stretched into the 200 model, which became Eastern's standard airplane on medium-haul routes. It was the world's most highly produced passenger jet until it was surpassed by the Boeing 737.

For its short-haul and lower-density flights, the company inaugurated DC-9 service in 1966 to critical acclaim (frustratingly the type was delayed several months because of production problems at Douglas). It was an important year in combating the obsolete piston predominance. Eastern put a total of 65 DC-9s and 727s on the line that year. It was a winning combination but couldn't immediately realize its full potential because the company was hit by a bitter machinists' strike that lasted a month and a half.

The mechanics struck five airlines simultaneously, but Eastern could least afford it due to its delicate financial position and high-cost/short-hop route structure.

This Eastern 649 Constellation demonstrates the limits of the aerodynamically effective and aesthetically gorgeous but snug fuselage. The protrusion below the fuselage is a speed pack to carry cargo for which there was no room onboard. It worked well because one could be preloaded and when the aircraft arrived the on board pack was detached for later unloading and the packed one was attached to send the airplane on its way expeditiously.

According to one senior Eastern executive, the company continued to suffer from three weaknesses even after the propliner equipment overkill problem had been solved: a high breakeven load factor caused by an essentially short-haul route structure, a high level of debt, and low historical profit margins compared to the rest of the industry. He should have also added an inability to carefully control expenses. These weaknesses would continue to haunt the company to the bitter end.

And in 1968 Eastern made another major financial commitment that would prove to be the beginning of the end. For $600 million, the largest order ever in its history, the company ordered 37 Lockheed L-1011s and optioned 17 more. The order was placed as the steadily growing passenger volumes nationwide took a turn for the worse because of a recession nobody had seen coming.

An Eastern Constellation seen at Milwaukee providing all coach service. The Connies finished their careers on the Eastern shuttle.

Eastern gave up its original DC-8 positions to wait for the model with the more powerful fanjet engines. Eastern was badly scooped by its competitor, Delta, that picked up the cancelled orders, but Eastern quickly regained lost ground when its own DC-8s arrived.

The L-1011 was chosen over the DC-10 in part because of Long Beach's problems in running its assembly lines, which had caused long delays on the DC-8s and DC-9s. However, the L-1011 also had a debilitating weakness in its Rolls-Royce RB-211 engines, putting it way behind schedule. The engines suffered from a design flaw in its fan-disk and quality control problems as the venerable engine maker was about to go into receivership. When the L-1011 entered service in late 1972, the problem hadn't yet been solved, and engine failure rates in service were high.

With the decreases in passenger volumes in 1968 and the need to service its high debt, Eastern was hit hard by a sharp decline in revenues. It did fly two leased Boeing 747s to compete with National's and Delta's 747s. Management correctly decided that they were too large for Eastern's routes to invest in them but felt compelled to meet the competition's challenge.

The situation didn't improve before the oil crisis hit, which especially affected the financially weak carriers from 1973 onward. An intercompany feud between the operations headquarters in Miami and the head office in New York further aggravated Eastern's woes.

Frank Borman was elected CEO in a last-ditch attempt to salvage the company, but he proved that it was easier to orbit the moon than run Eastern. The final nail in Eastern's coffin was deregulation and Frank Lorenzo. The airline raider saw a chance to get into the company relatively inexpensively, but the staff didn't roll over and take the massive salary cut he deemed crucial for Eastern to have a chance. Rocked by tumultuous internal turbulence, the company embarked on a feverish expansion to grab market share, even picking up bankrupt Braniff's South American routes. But as its financial woes mounted, a series of desperate strikes led to an impasse and the Great Silver Fleet went bankrupt, never to fly again.

Eastern was the launch customer for the Boeing 727, destined to become the world's best-selling airliner in its time. Its ability to use airports barely over 5,000 ft long with passenger loads greater than the B-720 and turn a profit on short- and medium-haul routes made it hard to beat.

CHAPTER 5

Trans World Airlines

I n the summer of 1957, TWA was about to send one of its latest Lockheed Constellations on a route-proving flight to Europe when it abruptly vanished. It fell victim not to an accident but to the whim of TWA's eccentric owner, Howard Hughes. The quirky billionaire commandeered the giant propliner for a six-month private Bahamian sojourn when it was desperately needed to duel with Pan American's DC-7Cs.

Hughes' cavalier use of the Constellation is revealing of his unique proprietary relationship with his airline. He had a passion for aviation and the airline business rivaled by few of his peers, and his immense wealth through the Hughes Tool Company allowed him to build up his ownership of TWA to 78 percent. But his hold over the airline was a mixed blessing.

He generously financed TWA from Hughes Tool Company's millions and played a leading part in creating the Lockheed Constellation and turning TWA into the first U.S. airline with an extensive domestic and international route network. But his absolute power also led him to make questionable decisions and allowed him to procrastinate when time was of the essence. In the end, he almost destroyed the airline that gave the world not only the Lockheed Constellation, but also the Douglas DC-1 and DC-2.

The airline Hughes would come to dominate for decades traces its lineage all the way back to the Darwinian menagerie of pioneering flying ventures from which America's airline system emerged in the 1930s. The driving force behind its evolution was Transcontinental Air Transport (TAT), formed in May 1928 for the sole purpose of providing coast-to-coast passenger air/rail service between New York and Los Angeles.

TAT was formed by the Clement Keys-controlled North American Aviation, that also held National Air Transport (which it would soon lose to United in a proxy raid) and Eastern Air Transport. Keys hired Charles Lindbergh to set up TAT's operations and publicized the ambitious new airline as "The Lindbergh Line."

TAT's two-day transcontinental service saved a day over going by train alone. It featured two overnight rail segments, between New York and Columbus, Ohio, on the Pennsylvania Railroad and Waynoka, Oklahoma, and Clovis, New Mexico, on the Santa Fe Railroad. TAT's Ford Trimotors flew the passengers the rest of the way.

It took more than a year to develop the infrastructure along the route, and three weeks before its inaugural trip on July 7, 1929, TAT was irritatingly scooped by Universal Aviation Corporation. The challenger's hastily assembled air/rail route had only one

Of all airliners, TWA is most closely associated with the Lockheed Constellations. The airline worked closely with Lockheed to create it and did its best to keep the initial model unavailable to competitors for as long as possible. This magnificent Constellation is a 1049H model restored and flown as a Super G by the Kansas City, Missouri-based Save A Connie Foundation. *Lawrence Feir*

TWA provided transcontinental service in the 1930s with Ford Trimotors when it was still known as Transcontinental and Western Airlines, following its merger with most of Western Air Express in 1930.

air segment between Cleveland, Ohio, and Garden City, Kansas, and took 19 hours longer than TAT.

Ultimately, neither venture provided a sufficiently better alternative to the express trains to attract enough passengers. And when only two months into scheduled operations a TAT Trimotor flew into Mt. Taylor in Arizona killing all on board, only a trickle of the most adventurous travelers went by air.

When TAT's air/rail service fizzled, Keys went for a foothold in the Southwest to lay the foundations of an air-only transcontinental service. He first acquired Maddux Air Lines, a tightly run, profitable operation flying the country's largest Ford Trimotor fleet between San Francisco, Los Angeles, San Diego, and Phoenix. It had carried more than 40,000 passengers in a year and a half after Jack Maddux, a dynamic Los Angeles car dealer had founded it, but Keys' offer proved irresistible.

TAT's second target, Harris "Pop" Hanshue's Western Air Express (WAE), was less cooperative. By 1930, Los Angeles-based WAE flew as far as Seattle, Salt Lake City, Kansas City, and Dallas, and Hanshue

had his own eye on reaching the East Coast. He rebuffed Keys, but shortly thereafter TAT got an unexpected boost from the U.S. government and Postmaster General Walter Folger Brown.

Brown brutally wielded the Watres-McNary Act to forge three viable, competitive transcontinental airlines and TAT was a winner, thanks to the Keys group's astute lobbying skills. Brown simply ordered Hanshue to merge the lion's share of WAE into TAT. The merged airline was called Transcontinental and Western Airlines, or TWA, and it shrank transcontinental airline travel to 27 hours, flying through the night.

With WAE came Jack Frye, who was quickly promoted to TWA's head of operations and would play a pivotal role in coming years. TWA also absorbed WAE's wooden winged Fokker F-10s, the type Lindbergh had rejected in favor of the all-metal Ford Trimotor.

On March 31, 1931, Lucky Lindy's judgment was tragically proven right when a TWA Fokker shed a wing in turbulence over Kansas, claiming the life of all on board, including Knute Rockne, Notre Dame's

TWA was also behind the creation of the Douglas DC-2, shown landing here, which led to the DC-3. Following the crash of a TWA Fokker, which claimed the life of Knute Rockne, football coach of Notre Dame, the airline submitted a request for a modern airliner and Douglas responded.

legendary football coach. The accident shook the airline industry to the core. The cause, moisture-induced wood rot of the wing spar, signaled the end of the wooden airliner. Developments in metal technology, stressed skin airframe construction, and cantilever wing design had been proven on smaller aircraft. The time had come to create the next generation all-metal airliner.

Jack Frye grounded the entire Fokker fleet (TWA went as far as burning some of them) and TWA's technical committee, headed by Charles Lindbergh set the requirements for the airliner's next airplane, which included all-metal construction, 14 seats, 180 miles per hour in cruise, three engines, and the ability to take off from any TWA airport on any two engines and safely fly the highest route in the system.

As TWA refined its specifications, word came of the Boeing 247. It had only 10 seats and only two engines, but its cruise speed of 160 miles per hour

would slash seven hours from TWA's 27-hour transcontinental route. United Airlines held the wonder plane's first 60 delivery slots.

In some desperation, Frye mailed TWA's specifications to five aircraft makers. Douglas Aircraft, a small-scale manufacturer from Santa Monica, California, with no metal airplane or mass production experience submitted the only serious response. What it lacked in experience, however, it made up in talent. Its chief engineer, James "Dutch" Kindelberger, headed one of the brightest young design teams in the business. They were cocksure they could top the Boeing 247 and Frye gave them the chance.

Like Boeing, Douglas discarded the antiquated trimotor concept in favor of a twin-engined configuration, and came up with a sleek, aerodynamic 12-seater, the Douglas Commercial One, or DC-1. Lindbergh specified that it had to be able to take off

Night flying was a routine operation by the mid-1930s. Here a TWA DC-3 is shown on a night stop. It is interesting to note that this aircraft is not a sleeper, indicated by the absence of top berth windows.

Airlines developed their own radio stations across their routes for communication and navigation. TWA had an extensive system of beacons on its transcontinental route, shown here in a passenger brochure to allay the concerns of nervous passengers.

on one engine from TWA's highest airport and safely climb over the highest obstacle in the system.

On July 1, 1933, the DC-1 took off on its maiden flight and almost crashed. As soon as it entered a sustained climb, the engines quit. As it leveled out, they would restart. Only Douglas chief test pilot Carl Cover's cool airmanship averted disaster. The problem turned out to be nothing more serious than carburetors installed backward.

The subsequent test flight program proved that the DC-1 exceeded the highest expectations. Most dramatic was the single-engine performance test out of Winslow, Arizona, the highest airport in TWA's network. Tommy Tomlinson, a highly talented former Maddux pilot was assisting Douglas test pilot Eddie Allen on the first single-engined test. The two had agreed that for the first takeoff Tomlinson would retard a throttle. Instead, he unexpectedly shut down an engine just before liftoff. The DC-1 performed flawlessly, as did a startled Eddie Allen.

TWA promptly ordered a stretched version, the DC-2, that allowed room for two more seats to meet the airline's 14-seat requirement. The TWA order for 25 airplanes was quickly followed by substantial orders from American Airlines and Eastern, setting off a flood of interest worldwide and sounding the death knell of the Boeing 247.

But as Douglas ramped up its production line, President Roosevelt shocked the industry by stripping the airlines of all their air mail contracts in the wake of Senate accusations of price fixing at the Republican spoils conferences. The mail was turned over to the U.S. Army, whose pilots were untrained for the task, and the result was disastrous.

Jack Frye used TWA's last air mail flight before the handover to demonstrate the Roosevelt administration's naiveté. As three Army fliers lay dead from crashes in bad weather on their way to their assigned air mail stations, Frye, with Eastern's Eddie Rickenbacker acting as his copilot, set a new transcontinental speed record in the DC-1. They flew from Burbank, California, to Newark, New Jersey, in 13 hours and 4 minutes, slogging their way through a massive blizzard on the last leg.

After five weeks and more dead army fliers, a chastened Roosevelt ordered the government to reopen the air mail for bids by the airlines under the Air Mail Act of 1934. Amidst some face-saving measures, TWA, like most of the airlines, won back its routes and Jack Frye was appointed president.

TWA's bigger, roomier DC-2s quickly established supremacy over the Boeing 247, beating it across the nation by as much as five hours. With the DC-2 came TWA's first stewardesses, or, as the company preferred to call them, hostesses.

But just as TWA was beginning to benefit from the DC-2's advantages, American stole a base on everyone by badgering Douglas into building the DC-3. With 14 sleeper berths in Douglas Sleeper Transport night configuration and 21 seats in day layout, it surpassed the DC-2 and only superficially resembled its predecessor.

TWA had to play catch up, introducing the DC-3 a full year behind American Airlines in June 1937. But catch up it did, and by then it was plotting greater plans. In Jack Frye's opinion, the airlines would truly come into their own only when they could carry passengers above most of the weather in pressurized comfort. And he was determined to have TWA lead the way.

At his behest, Tommy Tomlinson spent much of 1935 and 1936 exploring the air mass up to 40,000 feet in a sleek Northrop Gamma mail plane. He was the first to encounter the jet stream and the first to recognize that above 20,000 feet, an airplane can avoid most of the weather most of the time. His support for a high-altitude airliner was enthusiastic.

TWA participated in the United-led DC-4E consortium formed in 1936 to develop the modern four-engined airline, but based on Tomlinson's research, it was also talking to Boeing, which was still smarting from the 247 experience and was keen to get back into contention as an airline builder. Boeing engineers proposed turning the highly promising Boeing B-17 bomber into an airliner, the Boeing 307 Stratoliner.

TWA specified a pressurized cabin with room for 33 passengers in day configuration and 16 berths and 9 chaise-lounge chairs in night layout. The Stratoliner was to provide one-stop transcontinental service cruising as high as 20,000 feet, 30 knots faster than the DC-3. In early 1937, disenchanted with the DC-4E project (which would ultimately lead to the scaled-down, unpressurized DC-4), TWA signed a contract for six Stratoliners, closely followed by Pan American with an order for five.

The Stratoliner first flew on December 31, 1938, and by then TWA was embroiled in a major contract dispute with Boeing. It was engineered by TWA's largest stockholder, John Hertz (the Yellow Cab magnate and future car rental tycoon), who didn't share Frye's enthusiasm for the expensive airplanes because TWA had just lost almost a million dollars.

Another aircraft instigated by TWA was the Boeing Stratoliner, the world's first pressurized four-engined airliner. Following high-altitude research flights by a TWA Northrop Gamma, Jack Frye, the company's dynamic president concluded that airliners needed to fly above the weather to realize their full potential and worked with Boeing to develop the Stratoliner.

Pan American spun in on a demonstration flight for KLM. A dorsal fin, also adapted to the B-17, solved the problem and TWA put the type in service in July 1940, more than a year behind schedule.

The Stratoliner was loved by passengers, but it wasn't a commercial success. It was too small and slow to offset its operating costs and fell short of reliable one-stop transcontinental range. Conservatively cruising at 14,000 feet, its advantage over the DC-3 across the continent averaged a mere two hours. But it showed TWA the way and played a big part in motivating Frye and Hughes to pursue their next dream, which would become an enduring symbol of the golden age of propliners, the Lockheed Constellation.

When Frye and Hughes approached Lockheed with their requirements for a pressurized, four-engined, nonstop transcontinental airliner in 1938, the Burbank plane maker had one of the most innovative engineering departments, led by Hal Hibbard and Kelly Johnson (later of Skunk Works, U-2, and SR-71 fame). Lockheed was already working on the Excalibur, a 30-seat four-engined unpressurized landplane, for Pan American, and had also built a promising experimental pressurized version of the Electra, the XC-35.

By June 1939, Lockheed was ready with the preliminary design of project 0-49. Final details were hammered out in a series of marathon meetings, and in a matter of days, Hughes committed to buying 40 Constellations. He also set the pattern for the future handling of TWA's capital expenditures by buying the airplanes through the Hughes Tool Company, shielding TWA's fragile financials.

The Constellation was a masterpiece of aerodynamics, with a complex teardrop-shaped fuselage and upscaled P-38 fighter wings. Its triple vertical fins allowed it to fit into TWA's existing maintenance hangars, and,

These Trans World Airlines stewardesses in front of a Stratoliner are hamming it up, imitating the woman portrayed in the popular Petty poster encouraging everyone to do their part in World War II. TWA's Stratoliners certainly did. They served worldwide with Air Transport Command for the duration and all survived.

Hertz's short-term outlook clashed with Frye's strategic vision, and Hertz controlled TWA's board of directors. Frye was powerless and ultimately got so frustrated that he wanted out. With his most trusted colleague, he approached Howard Hughes, an acquaintance who had bought TWA's DC-1, and proposed that Hughes buy another airline they would run for him.

Sensing the chance to control a major airline, Hughes shocked them by deciding to buy TWA and cornered 25 percent of the stock to seize control. Frye and the Stratoliner deal were back on track and TWA was in for a long, wild roller coaster ride in the hands of the eccentric billionaire.

The Stratoliner suffered a tragic setback when one of the aircraft destined for

TWA's big victory prize at the end of World War II was becoming America's second major international airline behind Pan American, and it had the advantage of a domestic system that fed into its international routes. This postcard from 1946 showing a TWA DC-4 over Lake Geneva tells of exotic airline travel that was unimaginable to most Americans before the war.

according to Johnson, also aided yaw control. It had room for more than 50 seats, promised a service ceiling of over 25,000 feet, and was powered by aviation's most powerful powerplant, the 2,200-horsepower Wright R-3350, then still in the testing stage. At 20,000 feet, it would outrun the Curtiss P-40, one of the hottest fighters of the day. And it would slash in half the time it took to cross the continent.

TWA was convinced it would checkmate the competition. The unpressurized DC-4 was no threat and although the DC-6 was in the discussion stage, its production was way over the horizon. To further solidify TWA's competitive advantage, Hughes got Lockheed to commit to not even offering the Constellation to any other airline until the 35th one was delivered to TWA.

The obsessively secretive Hughes demanded total secrecy. The Constellation was built in a sanitized area foretelling the Skunk Works. At TWA only five people knew of it. TWA's liaison with Lockheed had a full-time cover job at Douglas of all places, as

Duel of the Piston Liners

The 1950s were characterized by the duel between Lockheed and Douglas to build the best piston-powered airliner. Even though the Constellation had the aerodynamically contoured, teardrop-shaped fuselage, the Douglas aircraft managed to retain a slight speed advantage from round to round. By the time the L-1649 and the DC-7C appeared, piston technology had reached its limits. There was nowhere to go but to the jets.

	First Service Date	Cruise Speed (mph)	Range (sm)	Gross Weight (lbs)	Passengers
L-049	1946	310	2,290	86,250	54
DC-6	1947	310	2,750	97,200	56
L-749A	1948	304	2,600	107,000	64
DC-6B	1951	315	3,000	107,000	66
L-1049G	1955	311	3,400	137,500	99
DC-7B	1955	360	2,800	126,000	99
L-1649	1957	342	6,000	156,000	99
DC-7C	1956	355	4,250	143,000	110

Source: R. E. G. Davies, *Airlines of the United States Since 1914.*

American Airlines and United, then already in negotiations for the DC-6.

But all the jostling for position among the airlines in the four-engined race was brought to an abrupt halt by World War II. The contenders would soon move up to four-engined transports, but they would be flying them for Uncle Sam. The war experience would be particularly generous to TWA. It would metamorphose into a major international airline in direct competition with Pan American.

TWA's five Stratoliners were the first to go. Gutted of their pressurization systems and loaded with auxiliary tanks, they were pressed into military transport and cargo service between Washington and Cairo via the South Atlantic, soon followed by service across the North Atlantic. TWA formed an Intercontinental Division to run its ATC flights, which became the cornerstone of the airline's postwar international operations.

Ironically TWA's Intercontinental Division was one of the first to be assigned the C-54, the military version for the DC-4. It also operated a Consolidated C-87 fleet, a cargo/passenger version of the B-24. TWA's state-of-the-art C-54s netted it a large share of VIP flights including flying President Roosevelt to the historic Casablanca and Yalta conferences. The war prompted the return of male flight attendants

the airline's DC-3 rep, sneaking off to Burbank only in the evenings and on weekends. Code names were used in communications. Hughes was God. Jack Frye was Jesus Christ.

The Constellation was forced to go public a few months before the Japanese attack on Pearl Harbor, when a War Production Board delegation assessing national aircraft production capability swooped into southern California. Its announcement was a national media sensation.

Justly feeling deceived in view of Lockheed's work on the now defunct Excalibur parallel with the Constellation, Juan Trippe indignantly demanded a matching order of Constellations for Pan American. Hughes relented, because he saw no threat from Pan American's international routes. But in exchange he got Lockheed to agree not to sell the Constellation to domestic transcontinental competitors, which effectively meant

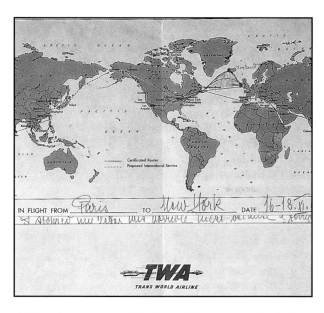

A French passenger's letter, written en route during a 1946 crossing from Paris to New York that took three days because of adverse weather. The real route taken via Iceland drawn in by the passenger is at odds with the optimistic direct route printed on the map.

The aft lounge featured on some Constellations. It was a challenge to make the space comfortable because of the fuselage's aerodynamic taper. Most Constellations had another, more convenient lounge area mid-fuselage.

into TWA's cabins, who stayed on in the Interncontinental Division after the war.

TWA's plans for the Constellation may have been put on hold by the war, but as allied troops were preparing for D-Day, Jack Frye and Howard Hughes managed to stage a forceful reminder of the postwar airline world to come. All Constellation production had been turned over to the military and the airplane was designated the C-69, but TWA was allowed to accept the first one and deliver it to the Army Air Force after the acceptance flights. On April 17, 1944, Frye and Hughes flew the prototype Constellation nonstop from Burbank to Washington, D.C., in a record-shattering 6 hours and 58 minutes.

The Air Corps was pleased by the publicity gained for America's air prowess but wasn't amused by the surprise TWA color scheme brazenly sloshed over the silver airliner with watercolors on the orders of Howard Hughes.

The flight symbolized the attention airlines were paying to the postwar world as victory was assured. For TWA, much of the focus was on the acquisition of international routes, aided by a Civil Aviation Board (CAB) determined to create more competition.

In mid-1944, TWA's efforts paid off. It won rights to Paris, Rome, Athens, Cairo, and with onward service to Bombay, India. Howard Hughes' airline became what Pan American could only dream of, an international carrier serving major global destinations fed by its extensive transcontinental domestic U.S. network.

As the war wound down, TWA and Pan American both took delivery of their first Constellations. Pan American was first across the Atlantic with the Connie, from New York to London, but TWA wasn't far behind. On February 5, 1946, the *Star of Paris* inaugurated the company's transatlantic Constellation service from Washington, D.C., to Paris via La Guardia. Ten days later, the *Star of California's* inaugural flight from Los Angeles to New York finally launched the service for which the Constellation was created.

As promised, the Constellation was fast, comfortable, and luxurious, but its range fell disappointingly short of nonstop transcontinental reach.

The Lockheed L-1649 was the last Constellation, which TWA called the Jetstream. It had a new wing and 6,000-mile range, but its operating costs were too high to make it more than marginally profitable, and it was overshadowed by the coming jets. As was common on propliners, the Jetstream's first class passengers rode in the back, away from the propellers.

All it could reliably manage nonstop was Los Angeles to Chicago.

Nevertheless, TWA's Constellations were riding high above the domestic competition's surplus C-54s. TWA was using aircraft everywhere, and all five Stratoliners even returned to the fold. But when the future looked rosiest, TWA was hit by a series of events in the second half of 1946 that severely jeopardized its competitive edge.

In July 1946, Howard Hughes crashed test flying the XF-11 high-speed reconnaissance airplane. He barely lived and was effectively out of action for months to come. A few days after Hughes' accident, a TWA Constellation on a training flight near Reading, Pennsylvania, caught fire and crashed, prompting the Civil Aeronautics Authority to ground the entire Constellation fleet. They stayed grounded for 69 days while the source of the fire was traced to a poorly designed electrical conductor that caused arcing. For much of the lucrative summer season, TWA's schedules were crippled by the grounding.

Barely a month after the Constellations were returned to service, TWA was hit by a bitter, five-week pilots' strike mandated by the Airline Pilots' Association to resolve crew duty and pay issues caused by the increasing sophistication of the four-engined airliners.

TWA could ill afford these setbacks. It had been spending lavishly to establish its European routes and maintain high service standards, and its problems were also compounded by an unexpected postwar recession that eroded optimistically anticipated passenger levels. TWA lost a record $14 million for 1946, and the stock price collapsed from $71 to $9.

Concurrently, Frye and Hughes fell out over funding TWA's capital expenditures. Frye favored selling more stock to raise capital while Hughes stuck to debt financing to prevent dilution of his ownership. The rift proved irreconcilable and in 1947, Jack Frye regretfully resigned.

An era had ended and the management vacuum caused by Frye's resignation wasn't adequately filled until 1949, a disservice the weakened airline felt acutely. In April 1947, barely more than a year after its introduction, the Constellation faced a formidable competitor, the larger, faster, and longer-range DC-6.

Lockheed already had an improved 649 Constellation on the assembly line that came closer to matching the DC-6, but TWA had to cancel its 18 orders

The contents of the onboard package awaiting Jetstream passengers. Among the postcards is a picture of a painting honoring Hollywood. It is one of a series of murals depicting TWA destinations commissioned to be displayed in the Jetstreams. *Martin Berinstein*

because of its financial difficulties. By the time it was ready to reconsider, Lockheed was offering the 749, which could compete effectively with the DC-6. In late 1947, TWA ordered 12 749s that were all put in service in 1948 and served mostly on the airline's international routes. They were soon followed by an order for 20 749As for delivery in 1950, the last and best variation of the original Constellation.

By 1950, the TWA roller coaster was zooming skyward again. The continuing financial success of the International Division and additional transcontinental Constellations had returned the airline to profitability. The company also gained important new European routes, and found a replacement airplane for its aging fleet of loyal DC-3s.

The European routes were recast when American sold American Overseas Airlines to Pan American. Intent on creating more competition, the CAB put TWA and Pan American head to head in London, Frankfurt, Paris, and Rome.

TWA was having financial problems that delayed the delivery of its Boeing 707s and threatened its competitive position. TWA managed to start transcontinental jet service a few months behind American Airlines with a sole 707, which made a daily round trip with clockwork reliability on its own for two months before additional 707 deliveries.

Closer to home, TWA found a DC-3 replacement to serve its web of feeder lines to its transcontinental services. Of the two contenders, the Convair 240 and the Martin 202, TWA had favored the Martin 202 back in 1947. But it had to postpone its decision because of financial constraints and was inadvertently saved from potential disaster when the 202's wing structural design weakness came to light in a tragic crash that almost bankrupted Northwest.

In 1949, when TWA returned to the market, Martin was offering the vastly improved pressurized 404, and Convair indicated a willingness to produce an improved Super 240. This time TWA selected the Convair, but at the last minute, Convair management reneged on developing the improvements. Stung by the rebuke, TWA switched to the Martin 404.

TWA signed up for 30 404s, later followed by an order for another 10. It also agreed to take 12 Martin 202As, unpressurized modified 202s, which were more immediately available. The first Martins went into service in late 1950 and the fleet served for a decade with only one fatal accident.

Transcontinental and Western Airlines marked the new decade with a name change to reflect its elevated postwar status. Henceforth it would be known as Trans World Airlines.

Meanwhile the duel of the four-engined propliners continued. Douglas matched the Lockheed Constellation 749A with the DC-6B, selected by both American and United. Efficient, fast, and more economical to build than the Connie because of its simple constant-width fuselage, it became the most productive four-engined propliner. Lockheed's response was to stretch the Connie into the 1049 Super Constellation.

The Super Constellation's 18-foot fuselage plug increased the airplane's passenger capacity to as many as 99, depending on configuration. It was to be powered by the 3,250-horsepower Turbo Compound version of the Wright R-3350 engine to keep pace with the DC-6B, but the engine wasn't available in time. Lockheed had to initially settle for 2,700-horsepower R-3350s and the airplane ended up being marginally slower than the DC-6B. Nevertheless, TWA, which had doubts about the reliability of the turbo compound engine, bought 10 Super Constellations, putting them in service in 1952.

TWA's next Super Constellations were the G models, the last in the series with the original wing, now equipped with the turbo-compounds. Entering service on April 1, 1955, TWA's Super Gs (as the airline called them) were its first true nonstop transcontinental airplanes and could also cross the Atlantic

TWA's Boeing 707s languish on the assembly line as the airline tries to sort out its financial problems. Howard Hughes' other major business, the Hughes Tool Company, which stood behind TWA's capital expenditures, hit severe financial turbulence and Hughes lost control of the airline to the creditor banks. The banks provided additional support to protect their own interests and 707 deliveries resumed.

nonstop in most weather conditions, although they lacked reliable New York–Paris range. They were a worthy match for the DC-7, Douglas' answer to the Super Constellation line, practically even in speed and featuring longer range.

In 1955, TWA was the first U.S. airline to introduce mixed first class and coach class flights, an innovation soon adopted industry-wide. Until the jets came, coach passengers rode in the noisier forward section of the propliners.

As the Super G entered service, the jets were around the corner and should have claimed Hughes' undivided attention. He was certainly intrigued, coming close to buying the Avro, a promising but little known Canadian jet that never went into production. But he was also concerned about the coming Douglas DC-7C, a long-range DC-7 with a stretched wing developed at Pan American's instigation, and was trying to decide what to make of turboprops.

Under pressure from the DC-7C, he made an equipment decision that would turn out to be an expensive misjudgment. Against sound advice, he bought the ultimate Constellation, the Lockheed 1649, a Super G fuselage mated to a brand new, high-performance wing, powered by 5,500-horsepower Pratt & Whitney turboprops. A military prototype, it looked like a sure winner over the piston DC-7C.

But soon after TWA's 25-airplane contract was signed, the turboprop engines encountered such technical difficulties that Pratt & Whitney cancelled the program. Instead of bailing out of the 1649 contract, Hughes agreed to substitute the latest R-3350 turbo compounds for the turboprops. If he couldn't beat the DC-7C, this revised 1649A would at least neutralize it. The Lockheed Starliner turned out to be overweight and slower than the DC-7C, but had unprecedented 6,000-mile range. The first Jetstreams, as TWA controversially called its Starliners, entered service in 1957, only a year and a half before Pan American's 707s launched U.S. airlines into the jet age.

Its days may have been numbered, but the Jetstream was immensely popular with its passengers.

It was the quietest piston airliner ever, its cabin was compartmentalized for a cozy, intimate effect, and its *piece de resistance* was the fully reclining Siesta Seat, at $2,500 a copy, arguably the best airline seat in the sky.

TWA wasn't ignoring the jets as Pan American, United, and American focused on the Boeing 707 and DC-8. It was zeroing in on another alternative. Howard Hughes was personally negotiating with Convair to build what he believed would be a bigger and better jet, the CV 18.

Ultimately Convair decided not to do the project because it rightly felt that the market was too small to sustain three similar models. TWA, however, had lost precious time. TWA was six months behind its main competitors when it ordered its first batch of eight Boeing 707s in March 1956. By January 1957 it had ordered a total of 33 707s, 15 -131s for domestic routes and 18 -331 Intercontinentals for foreign operations.

But more jets were needed to keep abreast of the competition. Hughes could have ordered more 707s, but once again he thought he had a better way to outfox his opponents. He was convinced that a smaller jet would be more economical on shorter routes and Convair was back with an exciting proposal for an 80-seat jetliner that would evolve into the CV 880. It promised to be the fastest airliner capable of crossing the continent. In addition to serving the shorter, thinner routes, Hughes also planned to operate it as the fastest, most exclusive first class transcontinental dash. In September 1956, he committed to 30 Convair 880s (concurrent with Delta's order for 40).

By the beginning of January 1957, the outlook was bright. TWA was preparing to face the jet age with a total of 63 jets on order. But the roller coaster had reached another crest. It was about to start heading down once again and this time Howard Hughes would fall off.

The problem was a change in the fortunes of Hughes Tool, the company that paid for TWA's aircraft. It was experiencing a major cash flow crisis and the aircraft lenders were getting nervous about their $125 million in outstanding loans. Hughes fought hard to forestall disaster. He cooked up excuses to delay aircraft deliveries, withheld progress payments from Boeing for spurious reasons, severely disrupted Convair's entire production schedule, and cut back TWA's pending jet fleet by 8 707-321s and 10 CV 880s. Aggravating the situation was Convair's less than stellar management of the CV 880 assembly line.

All this maneuvering, however, was invisible to the passengers as TWA blissfully inaugurated

transcontinental jet service with a sole Boeing 707 on March 20, 1959, between San Francisco and New York. TWA was only two months behind rival American, the first airline across the continent with jets. As more 707s entered the TWA fleet, it became evident that they were twice as productive as the Jetstreams.

TWA had its best financial year ever in 1959, primarily because of the jets, but the results couldn't come close to supporting the aircraft order backlog, and in the coming year, it found itself severely handicapped. It desperately needed more jets to compete, but no further Boeings were on order. Because of Hughes' financial difficulties it was anybody's guess when any of the Convair 880s would be delivered.

Following protracted negotiations, the banks finally made their move on December 29, 1960. They placed Hughes' TWA stock, which had grown to 78 percent of the company, in a 10-year voting trust, ousted him from all management control, and repossessed the TWA fleet.

TWA faced bankruptcy, but motivated by self-interest, the banks moved quickly to restore its financial health. By mid-1961, they authorized the purchase of 27 Boeing 707 fan-jets for $150 million,

The 80 seat Convair 880, promised to be the world's fastest, was a disappointment for TWA. The plan was to use it on high speed all first class transcontinental flights but it consumed so much gas at its top cruising speed that it couldn't make it across the country non-stop. It was used mostly on low density medium range routes.

The sheer size of the Boeing 747 is illustrated by this photo of a TWA crew getting its first look at the giant airliner. Note the competition's 747s across the way.

and got the Convair 880s delivered during the year. By 1962 TWA was again profitable, and over the next three years its stock soared from $7.50 to $97. But the jilted billionaire had the last word. When he finally sold his TWA stock, he pocketed $550 million.

As TWA recovered, it went all out to win customers with its impeccable service throughout its domestic and international network. Rosenthal china was featured on Royal Ambassador class, food service exceeded benchmark European transatlantic standards, and the airline was the first to introduce in-flight movies.

The Convair 880 was a disappointment, guzzling 7–10 percent more kerosene than predicted. It was more expensive to operate on medium-haul routes than alternative aircraft and never could make it across the continent at top speed with the first class elite. The quest for a medium-range jet continued and TWA, like practically every major U.S. airline, found salvation in the airplane that became the most successful jetliner in its time, the Boeing 727. TWA was behind launch customer Eastern and United in procuring the 727, but was operating more than 50 of the three-holers by the late 1960s with more on the way.

Thanks to its reversal of financial fortunes, TWA was also in on the ground floor with the icon of twentieth-century air transportation, the Boeing 747, ordering 12 of them in 1966. This order was followed by one for 22 Lockheed L-1011s, firmly

A TWA captain's coveted cap and uniform. At times he couldn't be sure how long he would continue to wear it as his airline's financial fortunes sagged, but in the end for most who made it into the left seat, their career was a rewarding ride. *Martin Berinstein*

committing TWA to the nascent widebody era. In 1967, the last Constellation was retired and TWA became an all-jet fleet.

The late 1960s were a heady time of international expansion. Service to Uganda, Kenya, and Tanzania commenced in 1967. TWA also received Pacific authority and went around the world in 1968 linking up with its long-standing Indian service via Europe. Motivated by synergy, the airline also bought the Hilton hotel chain.

But by 1971 the roller coaster that had peaked once again was about to head downward. A recession had taken hold and the enthusiastic abandon with which the airlines had been ordering jet equipment came home to roost in the form of over-capacity. The airlines' 747s were flying half empty on a good day, and TWA was particularly hard hit domestically because it had more competition on its route structure than the other airlines. On the international side, TWA cut services in Europe, gave up its short-lived round-the-world route, and its authority to Africa in a route swap with equally suffering Pan American.

And it was only the beginning. The 1973 oil crisis and raging inflation would soon take their toll and by 1975, TWA would have to sell some of its Boeing 747s to Iran just to meet its payroll. In the coming years, TWA would be ravaged by deregulation, watch other old-line trunk carriers disappear, and even go into protective bankruptcy. But in the end it would be a survivor, providing cheap, efficient, anonymous mass transportation on a level unimaginable to the crews of all those Trimotors, DC-2s, and Stratoliners.

Pan American

In the fall of 1928 Cy Caldwell, a former barnstormer, was passing through Miami on a ferry flight delivering a small, single-engined Fairchild float plane to Haiti when he was approached with an attractive proposition. Would he make a modest side trip for a large sum of cash? In good barnstorming tradition he acquiesced on the spot, and so, on October 19, 1927, he found himself lugging seven sacks of mail containing more than 30,000 envelopes from Key West to Havana, Cuba.

Caldwell couldn't have known it, but he had just flown the first trip of Pan American, the airline that would soon conquer the globe with its magical flying boats and in less than four decades would launch the Boeing 747. The airline needed his services on that fateful morning because it had a small problem. It held the air mail contract between Key West and Havana, it had leases on airfields in both places, and it had two brand-new Fokker F-VIIs. But the runway at Key West wasn't ready for use and time was running out. If no mail was flown on the route by day's end, the contract would lapse and Pan American would also forfeit a $25,000 bond.

Hastily hiring Caldwell to save the day was typical of Juan Trippe, Pan American's young president and general manager. The son of a well-connected New York family and a Yale alumnus, Trippe was obsessed with air travel and had been a principal in Boston-based Colonial Airways that held the Boston–New York air mail route and was eventually absorbed into American Airways. Trippe had left because Colonial's provincial principals weren't allowing him to expand the airline aggressively enough for his taste.

He turned his attention southward and won backing from his Wall Street friends for a new aviation adventure. His ambitions were global and given America's close business ties to the Caribbean and Central and South America during the 1920s, that is where he first set his sights. It was a tailor-made environment for air travel with its vast spaces, great tracts of water, marginal road and railroad network, and slow boats to palm-fringed harbors. In Trippe's pocket was a letter from Cuban dictator, General Machado that he had astutely acquired on a 1925 visit to the island, giving him sole landing rights in Havana.

The Pan American Airways Trippe was running the day it made its inaugural flight had been formed by the merger of three competing groups forced together by circumstance to secure the Key West–Havana air mail run. One group held leases to airfields in Key West and Havana and had good contacts in Washington but no airplanes. Another had access to additional financing to buy the airplanes. And Trippe held the trump card, the landing rights to Havana.

Passing the baton. A rare formation photo of a Pan American Boeing 707 and a Boeing 377 Stratocruiser. Although other piston propliners were more capable, for many passengers the Stratocruiser represented the high point of the piston era. The 707 became an equally potent symbol of jet travel.

At Pan American's Miami base, two flying boats wait for the next run to South America in the mid-1930s. In front is the four-engined Sikorsky S-40. Behind it is the twin-engined Consolidated Commodore inherited when Pan American acquired the New York–Rio–Buenos Aires line (NYRBA).

The runways were ready soon after the chartered Fairchild rescued the contract and on January 16, 1929, Pan American Airways flew its first scheduled passenger service with Captain Ed Musick at the controls of the shrewdly named *General Machado*, and four fare-paying passengers in the cabin. Trippe in the meantime was busy laying the groundwork for the next step of his global ambitions. He was in Washington, lobbying hard for his

M-28 AN AFTERNOON CROWD OF SIGHTSEERS AT PAN-AMERICAN TERMINAL, MIAMI, FLA.

SHOWING PORTION OF A 19 TON, 40 PASSENGER "CLIPPER"

PHOTO BY PAN-AMERICAN PHOTO SERVICE

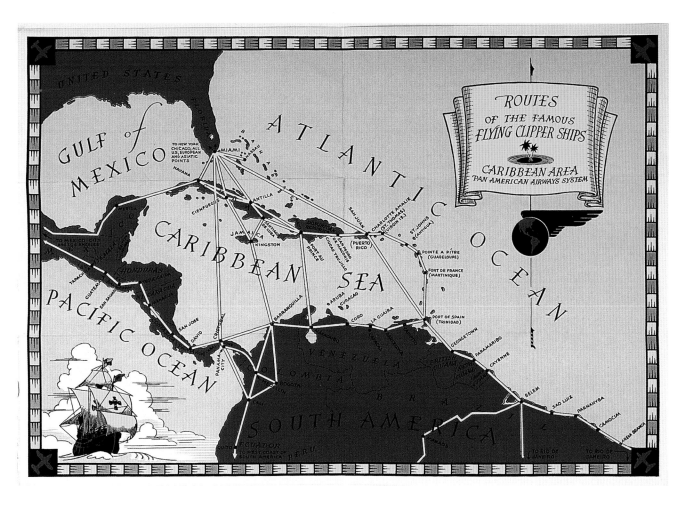

ROUTES
OF THE FAMOUS
FLYING CLIPPER SHIPS
CARIBBEAN AREA
PAN AMERICAN AIRWAYS SYSTEM

Within a few years of launching passenger service to Havana from Key West in 1929, Pan American's route network crisscrossed the Caribbean like a spider web.

vision of the future of American air transportation around the globe.

Few airline executives were better at lobbying Washington's powerful politicians and bureaucrats than Trippe. Underlying all efforts was the theme that in the national interest the U.S. government should favor a single airline to represent the United States abroad—Juan Trippe's Pan American Airways, the "Chosen Instrument" of American foreign policy.

This view was not as nearly as radical as it sounds today, for every other government followed the same policy, in practically all cases even outright owning and heavily subsidizing the national airline.

In part through Trippe's efforts, the 1928 Kelly Foreign Air Mail Act was worded to allow the postmaster general to select not the lowest bidder, but the one who in his opinion would "perform the service required to the best advantage of the government." Pan American was soon awarded two new air mail contracts, one from Cuba to Trinidad via Puerto Rico and the island chain beyond, and the other from Cuba to Panama through Central

America. Within a year, the company also had a route from Texas into Mexico.

Pan American was on its way. Trippe soon had Charles Lindbergh crisscrossing the region on survey flights and was opening up new opportunities deep into South America. Trippe unleashed his charm offensive on national authorities to smooth the way and where national laws prevented foreign carriers from operating in local skies, Pan American established local companies under its own control. In most locations, armies of Pan American construction crews created the necessary infrastructure and the airline's own ground personnel ran local operations.

The biggest challenge to Trippe's ambitious expansion plans along the West Coast of South America came not from any obstinate local dictatorship, but from an American adversary, W. R. Grace and Company. The giant trading and shipping concern considered the whole of western South America its own back yard and wanted in on any airline action proposed between it and the United States. Pan American, however, ruled the Central American

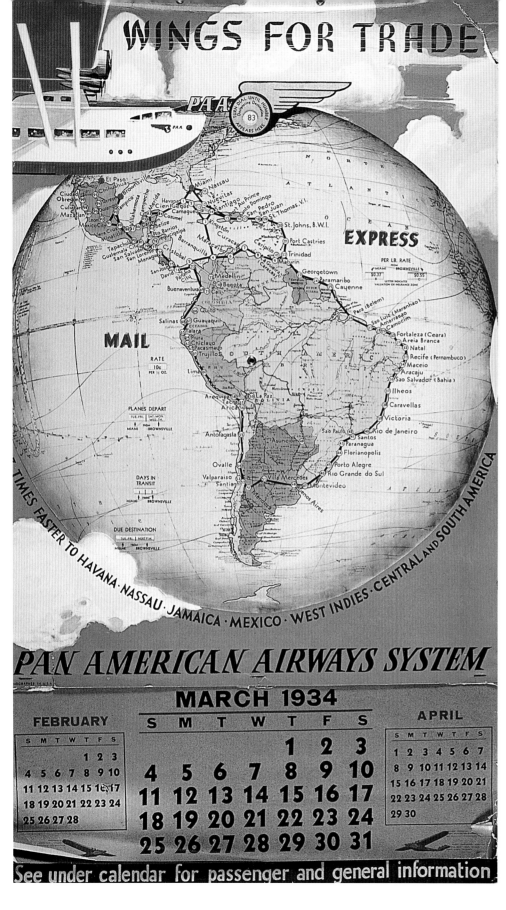

skies to the north, so Trippe made a deal. The two companies formed Pan American Grace Airways, or Panagra, a 50–50 joint venture to be managed by Pan American. When the ink dried on the agreement, Juan Trippe's air routes had grown by another 5,000 miles. In short order, he had the U.S. foreign air mail contract to go with it and even across the Andes from Chile to Argentina and Uruguay. But the Panagra marriage would prove to be a loveless one, as Pan American would consistently block Panagra's Grace-instigated attempts to fly to Central America and on to the United States.

As Pan American's Fokkers, Fairchilds, and Ford Trimotors fanned out across the spreading empire's land routes, it became obvious that on many of the over-water routes to coastal destinations, a capable flying boat was the best option. This realization led to the beginning of a strong association with Igor Sikorsky and his funky creations. Pan American put in service its first eight-seat Sikorsky S-38 amphibians in October 1928 and went on to buy another 37 of them, primarily for its Caribbean operations and to a lesser extent its subsidiary network.

In 1930, Juan Trippe realized another major objective. He closed the loop around South America by securing an eastern route down the coast to Rio de Janeiro and on to Buenos Aires. He did it not by pioneering the route but by acquiring a remarkable competitor, the New York, Rio, and Buenos Aires line, or NYRBA.

Founded only two years before by Ralph O'Neill, a former Boeing marketing rep and highly decorated World War I pilot, it was initially well capitalized by Wall Street backers and operated 11 elegant 22-seat Consolidated Commodore flying boats between Florida and Buenos Aires, locally augmented by a fleet of S-38s. It was every bit as credible an operation as Pan American, but it was vulnerable. It had no U.S. foreign air mail contracts and was losing money. Its backers were increasingly feeling the financial chill of the stock market crash and were reluctant to provide further support to NYRBA. Only the U.S. air mail contract would help, but O'Neill was unknown in Washington. When he applied, he was advised to sell out to Pan American.

An intriguing Pan American office wall calendar that allows the user by twirling the disk under the globe to tell at a glance the schedules, days in transit, and cost of express mail to any destination in the Pan Am system.

The 34-passenger, 150-miles per hour Sikorsky S-42 served South America and Bermuda and flew proving flights across the Pacific and the Atlantic. In scheduled Pacific service, S-42Bs flew the Manila–Hong Kong segment and the entire South Pacific route to New Zealand. The famed Captain Musick and his crew were lost in the crash of an S-42B off Pago Pago in 1938.

As soon as Pan American completed the buyout, it was awarded the air mail route to Buenos Aires. In only three years, Trippe had grown Pan American from one 90-mile route and two eight-seat Fokkers into a major carrier with over 20,000 miles of routes through 20 countries flown by dozens of airplanes and flying boats. And the boats were getting bigger.

Pan American's next Sikorsky was the S-40, with four engines and 38 seats, over twice the size of the S-38. The S-40 was the first Pan American aircraft to be called a *Clipper* to evoke the romance and achievements of America's swift, long-distance sailing ships of a century before. The name would be on the nose of every Pan American aircraft from then on and would capture the imagination of tens of millions of passengers.

Three S-40s were built, but even as the first one, the *Clipper America*, took off on its maiden revenue flight from Miami to Panama with Charles Lindbergh at the controls in November 1931, Juan Trippe was plotting longer-range, larger flying boats. In its extensive Latin American network, Pan American now had the bread-and-butter business that allowed him to turn his attention to spanning oceans on a schedule.

Trippe would have liked to pioneer the passenger routes across the Atlantic first, but British resistance to the commencement of American service before Britain was able to reciprocate and blocked his attempts. He therefore set out to conquer the Pacific and launched one of civilian aviation's most audacious and romantic adventures.

A 1931 survey flight by Charles Lindbergh and his wife to the Far East via Alaska indicated that the route was technically suitable with relatively brief over-ocean legs. But a belligerent Soviet Union, and a militant Japan about to invade Manchuria barred the way. The only option was across the vast central Pacific from San Francisco to Hawaii, then on to the two tiny specs of Midway and Wake, then to Guam and Manila, and up to Hong Kong. The total distance was 7,500 miles, the longest leg 2,400 miles between San Francisco and Hawaii.

Trippe had two ultra-long range-flying boats on order for the task, the Sikorsky S-42 and the Martin M-130. The S-42 was first to join Pan American's fleet and was the boat which would prove conclusively that aviation technology had come far enough by the 1930s to provide scheduled transoceanic passenger service.

November 22, 1935.
Pan American's Martin
M-130 *China Clipper*
with Captain Ed Musick
in command departs
San Francisco on the
first scheduled
transpacific air mail
flight. The next stop is
Hawaii, the final
destination Manila,
Philippines. Passengers
wouldn't be carried for
another year.

It had room for a maximum of 32 passengers, was more luxurious than any landplane, and its 2,500-mile range gave it unprecedented reach. While in standard configuration, it fell just short of reliable transpacific range along the contemplated route segments; with auxiliary fuel tanks, it became Pan American's pivotal route survey plane. And even as it was being readied for its long-range surveys, Pan American was awaiting delivery of the Martin M-130, a four-engined 41-seat flying boat with 3,200-mile range, more than enough for any leg of the Pacific crossing.

Trippe was confident that he had the flying boats to do the job, but before the survey flights could get underway, another technological breakthrough was needed. Navigating across the oceans was so demanding, the margin for error so narrow, that the traditional tools of dead reckoning and celestial navigation couldn't be counted on to reliably provide the margin of safety required for scheduled service.

The problem was solved by Hugo Leuteritz, Pan American's chief communications engineer, who developed a long-range radio direction finder effective out to 1,200 miles. As the aircraft transmitted, the ground station got a bearing on it and relayed the information back to the aircraft. It was a major technological advance, although the unreliability of electronic equipment in those pre-solid-state days was nevertheless to cause many a tense moment in the cockpit in coming years.

Equipped with extra tanks, the S-42 *Pan American Clipper* was repositioned to San Francisco in the spring of 1935. An intense period of training flights followed, focusing on navigation, including riding Leuteritz's radio beam, and on monitoring aircraft performance and fuel consumption.

On the afternoon of April 16, 1935, with Captain Ed Musick in command the *Pan American Clipper* headed westward out of San Francisco, flew into the sunset and arrived in Honolulu the next morning.

The first step was complete. But instead of pushing on, the plan was to return to San Francisco. Pan American would build up to the full crossing in careful, methodical stages. The return flight four days later ran into stiff headwinds, graphically reminding the crew of their undertaking's potential perils. The S-42 was estimated to have an endurance of 21 hours. When they touched down in San Francisco bay the next afternoon, they had been airborne for 23

The map is of an actual transpacific crossing used as a learning aid in *Weems' Air Navigation*, the standard textbook on the subject in the late 1930s. Note the use of DF radio bearings in addition to celestial bearings to establish the aircraft's position, especially as it gets close to an island destination. The model is a Martin M-130 flying boat. The flight attendant pins portray Pan American's South American presence. *Martin Berinstein*

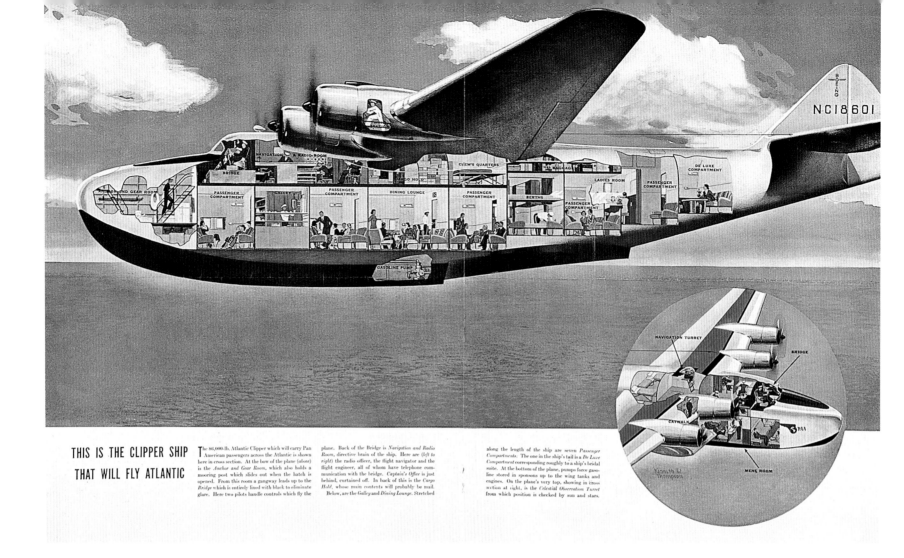

THIS IS THE CLIPPER SHIP THAT WILL FLY ATLANTIC

The 86,000-lb. Atlantic Clipper which will carry Pan American passengers across the Atlantic is shown here in cross section. At the bow of the plane (above) is the *Anchor and Gear Room*, which also holds a mooring post which slides out when the hatch is opened. From this room a gangway leads up to the *Bridge* which is entirely lined with black to eliminate glare. Here two pilots handle controls which fly the plane. Back of the Bridge is *Navigation and Radio Room*, directive brain of the ship. Here are (left to right) the radio officer, the flight navigator and the flight engineer, all of whom have telephone communication with the bridge. *Captain's Office* is just behind, curtained off. In back of this is the *Cargo Hold*, whose main contents will probably be mail. Below, are the *Galley* and *Dining Lounge*. Stretched along the length of the ship are seven *Passenger Compartments*. The one in the ship's tail is a *De Luxe Compartment* corresponding roughly to a ship's bridal suite. At the bottom of the plane, pumps force gasoline stored in sponsons up to the wing tanks and engines. On the plane's very top, showing in cross section at right, is the *Celestial Observation Turret* from which position is checked by sun and stars.

The interior details of the ultimate passenger flying boat, the Boeing 314. A true double-decker, its upper deck was the crew's domain. The passenger compartments and the dining lounge resembled the comforts of a luxury train. The seats converted to berths for the night. Crossing the Pacific in the aft private suite was surely the most extravagant air travel experience. Note the in-flight access to the engines.

hours and 14 minutes and the bottom of the fuel tanks was barely damp.

Other proving flights followed. Pan American engineering crews constructed ground facilities en route, and the company took delivery of the first Martin M-130.

Trippe and the flight crews were generally satisfied with the survey results and decided to make their move. Christened the *China Clipper*, the new Martin set out from San Francisco for Manila on November 22, 1935, on the first scheduled transpacific air mail flight. Its tumultuous sendoff was a nationally broadcast event and in Manila, it was met by a crowd of 300,000. By journey's end Captain Ed Musick was a national hero, and Juan Trippe had fulfilled one of his most cherished dreams.

Passengers weren't carried for another year as Pan American built experience flying the mail and built hotels along the way to accommodate its passengers. But on October 21, 1936, the *Philippine Clipper*

took off from San Francisco and arrived in Hong Kong three days later with 15 fare-paying passengers on board. The clippers had shrunk the transpacific crossing from three weeks to three days.

In 1937 Juan Trippe was awarded the Collier Trophy, U.S. aviation's highest honor, for establishing transpacific passenger service. But the aerial thread linking the two continents was tenuous. Pan American had only three Martins on the route augmented by an S-42B, an improved, longer-range version of the S-42. In spite of this meager fleet, Trippe had pushed through a second route down to New Zealand. And then disaster struck. First, in January 1938, the S-42 *Samoan Clipper* blew up near Pago Pago killing the legendary Captain Musick and his crew and in July that year, the *Hawaiian Clipper* disappeared without a trace between Guam and Manila.

The transpacific schedule had to be cut, the New Zealand route was suspended, and Pan American was losing money on the remaining route. But

Trippe pushed on. Three months before the *Philippine Clipper's* historic passenger flight he had committed more than $3 million to the biggest, most luxurious flying boat of all, the Boeing 314. Six were on order and the first deliveries were imminent. The first two would take the pressure off the Pacific and for the rest Trippe had plans across the Atlantic.

The B-314 had no peer. Twice the size of the Martin M-130, with a gross weight of 40 tons, it was the biggest commercial aircraft until the advent of the Boeing 747. It could carry 74 passengers in day configuration or 40, equipped with sleeping berths. Its comfortable lounges, dining room, and deluxe private suite in the back were never again to be seen on a scheduled passenger airliner. And it was the first to establish regular passenger service across the Atlantic.

While it was making headlines with its ocean-roving flying boats, Pan American hadn't ignored landplane developments, important in the short run for its Latin American routes and in the long run for its global ambitions. The company was behind the major domestic U.S. airlines to buy the DC-2, but it ordered 19 of them to serve its affiliate companies. Pan American also bought the DC-3, taking delivery of 49 aircraft between 1937 and 1942.

As more complex land-based airliners appeared, Pan American understood that they spelled the end of the flying boat and kept its bets covered. The company signed up for the first pressurized airliner, the Boeing 307 Stratoliner, and participated in the consortium funding the DC-4's development, ordering 28 of the final design. The Stratoliners briefly entered service but none of the DC-4s were delivered before both types were diverted for wartime service along with a large segment of the rest of Pan American's fleet.

Most significantly in 1940 with great foresight, Pan American ordered 40 Lockheed Constellations (after it found out that they were being secretly built for Howard Hughes' TWA, and sternly demanded its fair share). The swift, sleek, pressurized airplane would decisively seize the competitive edge in the immediate aftermath of World War II and lead the way in redefining international air travel.

As the Constellation order was negotiated, Pan American was grappling with a problem it had hoped never to face—the first real threat to its global hegemony. The interloper was the American Export Line shipping company, which had decided to start up a flying boat subsidiary and get into the transatlantic airline business.

To Pan American's horror, the CAB approved the application as pressure in Congress grew to provide

A flying boat navigator shooting a star with a sextant to determine the aircraft's position. The risk of encountering overcast skies was considered too large to launch scheduled transoceanic service relying only on the stars, so Hugo Leuteritz, Pan American's chief communications engineer, perfected long-range radio navigation to tackle the oceans. During World War II, however, when strict radio silence had to be maintained, crossings were routinely made on celestial navigation alone.

PAA

Routes of the Flying Clipper Ships

[AS OF DECEMBER 7, 1941 · SUBSEQUENT WARTIME CHANGES CENSORED]

PAN AMERICAN WORLD AIRWAYS

"Wings of Democracy"

By 1941 Pan American spanned both the Pacific and the Atlantic. The flying boats still got all the global glamour, but the Boeing 307 Stratoliner in the upper right corner of the map signaled the flying boat's final days.

Pan American some competition. Pan Am fought the ruling on the grounds that it was anticompetitive for a shipping line to own an airline. Pan Am eventually prevailed, but the victory in 1945 was double edged because the court-ordered divestiture gave American Airlines majority control in what became American Overseas Airlines (AOA).

As the biggest airline with the largest international network in the world, Pan American's contribution to the war effort was greater than that of any other airline. Its flying boats and landplanes provided regular transatlantic and transpacific service along the routes the company

had pioneered. Its flight crews and ground personnel pushed those routes further, particularly the long supply bridge from Brazil across the South Atlantic through Africa into Asia, and the marathon route down to Australia.

The war's end held great promise for Pan American as capable new landplanes with global reach proven in war were about to become available for commercial airline service. Especially attractive was the prospect of air service to Europe. But Pan American was also facing a serious challenge to its predominance. After opening the door across the Atlantic with AOA, the U.S. government was about

The *Yankee Clipper* flew the first scheduled transatlantic flight along the southern route from New York to Marseilles via the Azores and Lisbon on May 20, 1939, and along the northern route to Southampton, England, via Shediac and Botwood, Canada, and Foynes, Ireland, on June 24, 1939.

A commemorative letter from onboard the first Northern transatlantic scheduled flight flown on June 24, 1939.

to allow the domestic U.S. carriers to bid on international routes on a larger scale.

Pan American was hopeful that in exchange, the government would allow it to bid on domestic rights. But it was not to be. Pan American was judged to be so powerful that it would never gain domestic access under regulation.

Over the Atlantic, Pan American found itself facing Trans World Airlines in addition to AOA. In July 1945, Pan American was awarded rights on the route to London, southern Germany, Istanbul, Tehran, Karachi, and Calcutta, but Trans World Airlines got the Paris, Rome, Athens, Cairo, and Bombay route. AOA was to compete with Pan American to London, and would go on to Scandinavia and northern Germany.

Pan American's Pacific monopoly was infringed by route awards to United and Northwest. United was to share the lucrative route to Honolulu, and Northwest, which had given such outstanding war service in the forbidding Alaskan environment and beyond, was given the northern route to the far east via Seattle and Anchorage.

And Pan American wasn't even safe in its biggest stronghold, Latin America. National and Braniff both got a toehold in Havana, and the Truman administration practically commanded

No contemporary scheduled aircraft could match the dining rooms of the Boeing 314. Onboard cooking equipment enabled the preparation of fairly elaborate menus by the day's culinary standards that included such items as breaded veal cutlets with paprika sauce and whipped potatoes. Note the prominently displayed milk and soft drinks at the front table while the steward serves wine in the background.

Braniff to fly to Mexico City, Rio de Janeiro, and Buenos Aires in competition with Panagra.

But regardless of Trippe's grousing, by modern standards of cutthroat competition the controlled route awards to competitors left plenty of business for Pan American to ensure its position as America's preeminent international airline.

As postwar airline services got underway, Pan American's prestige was tweaked by newcomer American Overseas Airlines. On October 24, 1945, an AOA DC-4 flew the first scheduled landplane crossing of the Atlantic cutting in half the Boeing flying boat's crossing time.

But Pan American had long stopped counting on the flying boat as the ideal way to cross. The *Bermuda Clipper's* 1945 Christmas flight from Lisbon to New York was the end of transatlantic flying boat service, and on January 20, 1946, Pan American was the first to cross in scheduled service with the technologically most advanced airliner of the day, the Lockheed

Constellation. Shortly thereafter, a Pan American Constellation also completed the first ever scheduled around-the-world flight.

Starting in late 1945, Pan American also took delivery of large numbers of DC-4s, eventually operating 92 of them throughout its system. The DC-4 brought down the final curtain on the Boeing flying boats in the Pacific. It also introduced coach class on the New York–San Juan run in 1948, to compete with the fire sale prices of charter operators, a service that proved to be a spectacular success. Passenger volume on the route increased fivefold in a few months. Coach class, forced on the scheduled carriers by the mushrooming charter companies, was hard to swallow for an industry so proud of its glamorous image. But Juan Trippe, with his obsession to put the whole world on Pan American, was a staunch supporter of the concept from the beginning.

Even before the first Pan American Constellation crossed the Atlantic, Trippe had ordered the landplane that would best emulate the luxury of the disappearing flying boats, the Boeing 377 Stratocruiser. Looking like a fattened-up B-29 (which it essentially was), it went into service with Pan American in 1950. Its spacious cabin, the cozy downstairs bar, and a private suite were instant hits with passengers, but its unreliable engines drove pilots to distraction, and it was expensive to operate. Not a great economic success, it had a good run because of its unmatched level of luxury service.

In 1952 Pan American introduced the first of its 45 DC-6Bs, Douglas' somewhat belated answer to the Lockheed Constellation. The DC-6B was the most economical piston-engined airliner ever built, and Pan American bought them with economy in mind. Following its success with coach class between New York and Puerto Rico, the airline was keen to try the concept across the Atlantic. The first DC-6Bs launched tourist class service between New York and London, packed with 82 seats, aptly named Rainbow Service. The DC-6B went on to excel in all classes and served until 1968, some of the last of them gallantly flying Pan American's shuttle through the Berlin air corridors.

Pan American was the lead instigator of the last big propliner it bought, the DC-7C, nicknamed the Seven Seas. It was the first airliner capable of crossing the Atlantic nonstop in scheduled service, but its days were numbered even as it was introduced in 1957. The high-pitched howl of a jet was replacing the thundering of pistons as the most thrilling sound in the sky, and within a year, Pan American would take delivery of its first Boeing 707.

As early as 1949, Boeing invited Pan American to help fund the development of a long-range jetliner, but the amounts required were too large and the outcome at that stage too uncertain to win a commitment. Boeing gambled on its own (also gunning for the U.S. Air Force aerial tanker contract) and by 1954, it flew the Dash 80, the prototype 707.

In principle Trippe was hooked on jets, but was initially cool to the 707, deeming it too small and underpowered, and objecting to its lack of true transatlantic range. Pan American was also in close touch with Douglas who had started preliminary development of the DC-8, and the horse trading began. Trippe and his lieutenants mercilessly cajoled both manufacturers to make their jets bigger and badgered Pratt & Whitney into making the bigger, more fuel-efficient engine available.

Douglas was the first to give in. Having only a paper airplane it was in a better position to revise its initial design. Trippe, however, still wanted a jet as

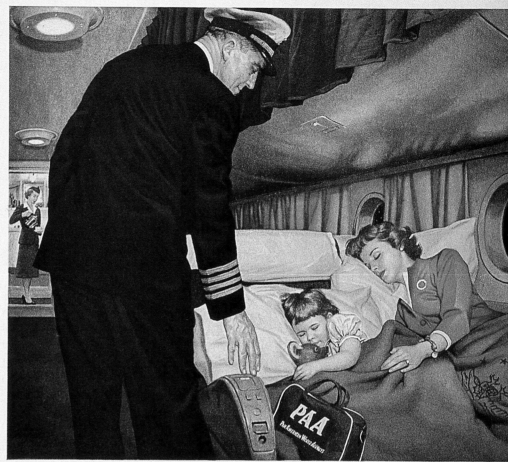

Not all seats converted to berths on most Stratocruiser flights. Sections of lower seats simply reclined similar to modern first class seats. In the 1950s the image of the experienced captain watching over the sleeping child played powerfully on the safety theme.

This Stratocruiser swoops lower than normal over London's Tower Bridge, catching a similar view seen by today's jets on arrival at Heathrow if the aircraft circles the city landing to the west.

soon as possible and the 707 was available earlier. And he was convinced that a little pressure would ultimately get Boeing to revise its design.

He signed a contract for 20 Boeing 707s, and Boeing executives anxiously awaited the official announcement. But when it came out on October 13, 1955, they were in for a nasty shock. Pan American had simultaneously ordered 25 Douglas DC-8s. Boeing was five orders down to a paper airplane.

At this stage, Pan American benefited from the actions of United who also ordered the DC-8 and American who bluntly told Boeing it wouldn't buy the 707 unless the fuselage was widened by a foot to match the DC-8. Now it was Boeing's turn to relent. American placed its order, and Pan American's was revised. Trippe had his fuselage. He would accept the first six 707s with the smaller engines, but the rest would come with the one he had wanted all along.

On October 26, 1958, the *Clipper America's* four jet turbines thrusted it skyward with an ear-splitting whine from New York's Idlewild airport. Its 111 passengers, 40 in first class and 71 in economy, were on their way to Paris at twice the speed of the fastest piston propliner, aboard the first scheduled jet service by an American airline. Today, over four decades later, the most modern jetliners have longer range but are only marginally faster.

The DC-8 entered service 16 months later. Pan American eventually reduced its DC-8 order to 19 and never bought another Douglas airplane (the DC-10s it operated in the 1980s were inherited when it acquired National).

The jets were the stars of the 1960s. Pan American was the international jet set's most potent symbol, and the world's dominant airline. Pan American bought 137 707s in all, including nine shorter-range 720Bs for its Latin American routes. The company also bought 25 727s for its Caribbean routes and its service between West Germany and Berlin. But Juan Trippe wasn't slowing down to reflect on how far Pan American had come since that first mail hop from Key West to Havana with a borrowed floatplane. He was badgering Boeing, plotting his last and most spectacular deal.

During the first half of the 1960s, international passenger traffic was growing at a phenomenal 25 percent every year. At that rate, the current jet types would have a hard time keeping up with demand. Concurrently Lockheed and Boeing were competing to build a mammoth cargo plane for the U.S. Air Force. Trippe, whose ideal airliner had always been an ocean liner of the air, concluded that the time had come for the ultimate passenger jet. It would be a

A short-bodied Constellation of Panair do Brasil, one of many local South American airlines founded and controlled by Pan American. Local companies controlled by Pan American had an important role in the foundation of air travel in Latin America. They were eventually sold to local owners, many of them in the mid-1960s as the countries became less beholden to U.S. business interests.

behemoth motivated by nothing more than Trippe's obsession to maximize passenger volume, but it would become one of the most potent icons of twentieth-century technical achievement.

As Trippe fleshed out his vision, Boeing lost the Air Force cargo plane contract to Lockheed's C-5A Galaxy and refocused its attention on developing an airliner of similar size, a cause passionately seized by Juan Trippe. Pan American and Boeing worked together to lay out the giant's specifications. It would carry 450 passengers (two and a half times the number on the 707) over 5,000 miles, at 35,000 feet, above Mach .80. Its efficient turbofans and its economies of scale would make it over 30 percent more economical to operate than the 707 and the DC-8.

Project 747 would cost Boeing more than $2 billion to develop, and such a commitment demanded a sizeable order up front. Based on passenger volume projections, Pan American was ready to oblige. On December 22, 1965, Juan Trippe and Boeing's Bill Allen signed an order for 25 Boeing 747s worth $550

The Stratocruiser's downstairs bar was its most talked about feature. It was created in part at the instigation of Pan American to capture the atmosphere of the flying boat lounges for which there was little room on the new, streamlined landplanes.

In 1957 Pan American needed to raise enormous amounts of capital to pay for its massive order of Boeing and Douglas jetliners and other capital expenditures. One of Juan Trippe's skills was his ability to convince Wall Street to finance Pan Am.

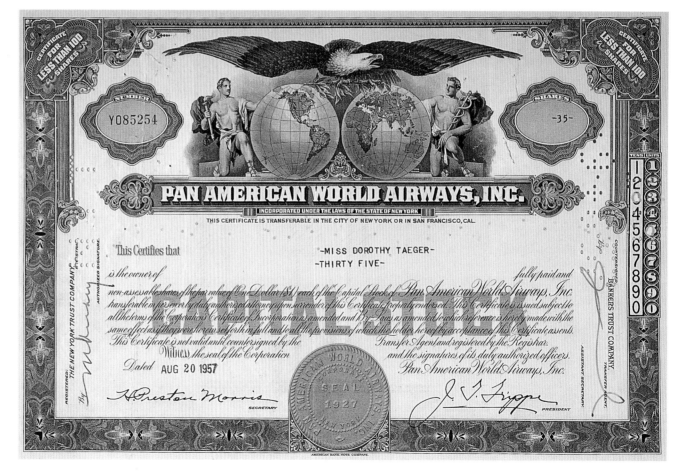

Pan America was the airline behind the creation of the Boeing 747. Juan Trippe bet
$500 million on 25 747s, and Boeing bet $2 million on the development costs. Had the
747 been a failure, it would have bankrupted both companies.

Pan Am debuted Clipper Class menus to commemorate significant firsts accomplished by the airline over its tumultuous life. The first scheduled passenger flight across the Pacific and the Atlantic, the first scheduled U.S. passenger jet flight and first scheduled flight of the Boeing 707, and the first scheduled flight of the Boeing 747. The cover of this one depicts a Boeing 314 lifting off on a flight across the Pacific.

CLIPPER CLASS

Welcome Aboard Pan Am's Special Business Class

Libations

Aperitifs   Cocktails   Spirits   Red and White Wines
Champagne   Premium Beer   Liqueurs and Cognac

Menu

Cocktail Nuts

Délice Fleurette Salad
Smoked Nova Scotia salmon on a bed of fresh greens with savoury garnishes

Veal Scallopini Mediterranean
Medallions of Veal in a light cream sauce.
Served with spätzle

or

Chicken Kiev
Tender breast of chicken with a seasoned butter filling baked golden brown.
Served with glazed Belgium carrots and buttered snow pea pods

Blueberry Cheesecake
Fresh baked New York style cheesecake

Continental Breakfast

French Croissant

Blueberry Crumb Cake

Creamery Butter

Coffee   Taster's Choice Decaffeinated Coffee   Tea
Coca-Cola   Canada Dry Beverages   Pepsi Cola
Diet Coke   Diet Pepsi
Caffeine Free Diet Coke   Diet Pepsi Free
Country Time® Lemonade Flavor Drink

Please accept our apology if your choice is not available.

6590
4-1-96

million. Pan American would have to pay half the amount even before the delivery of the first 747, scheduled for 1969. The two men had bet their respective companies. Failure would mean bankruptcy.

The 747 project did not get off to a good start. As the design progressed, it gained weight at an alarming rate. By mid-1967, its maximum gross weight was at 710,000 pounds, up 23 percent from the contractually committed figure of 550,000 pounds. Boeing suggested accepting a decrease in performance and passenger capacity or delaying the project until more powerful engines could be developed. Trippe would tolerate no delay. He cajoled Boeing to put the 747 on a severe diet and pestered Pratt & Whitney for more power.

Ultimately the solution was compromise, similar to the earlier experience with the Boeing 707. The airplane lost weight and came closer to its promised performance, but it would initially carry 367 passengers instead of 450. More powerful engines that would achieve performance specifications would be available, but not for three years after the first 747s entered service.

In 1968, with the 747 well on the way, Juan Trippe finally retired, the last to go of the five airline titans who formed the industry. The behemoth that was his legacy lifted off for the first time on February 19, 1969, and Pan American intended to inaugurate it by year-end. The flight tests went well, except for a variety of engine problems, which were prone to overheating. Annoyingly, Pan American's inaugural evening flight from New York to London, scheduled for January 21, 1970, had an engine overheat as it taxied onto the runway at JFK. The *Clipper Young America* didn't get underway until 1:52 A.M. the following morning.

Those of a superstitious bent would have been right to interpret the 747's rocky inaugural as a bad omen. While the giant jetliner would work through its teething problems to become one of the most reliable aircraft ever, the airlines were in for a rough ride because the optimistic projections of the mid-sixties had become meaningless. As recession gripped the economy, the rosily forecast flood of passengers evaporated. Acres of empty 747 seats wandered the sky as their operators' profits hemorrhaged. The cavernous empty interiors were turned into piano bars, lounges for all classes, and even onboard restaurants to attract passengers, but to no avail.

Pan American was particularly badly hit. Its former lion's share of the lucrative North Atlantic traffic was down to a mere 7.5 percent by the late 1960s as scores of government-owned and supported foreign airlines insisted on flying the prestige run. Matters

Today's passengers are used to the size of the widebodies, but to the first passengers, the widebodies were awesome. Note how the ad emphasizes spaciousness with the passengers spread out in the front row, and the glamour of air travel with the young lady heading up the circular stairs to the lounge.

Initially Pan American was not a big Boeing 727 user, but the airplane filled important niches in Caribbean service for the airline and on its Berlin Shuttle.

weren't much better over the Pacific, and the CAB relentlessly continued to deny Pan Am any domestic routes that could have at least eased the problem. In Latin America, the feud between Pan Am and its partner, W. R. Grace and Company became so intense that they were forced to sell Panagra to Braniff.

Compounding Pan American's woes was its staggering $600 million debt load. Within three years

The coffee cup and saucer flew on Pan American's Boeing flying boats in the 1940s. The stewardess uniform is from the 1950s. The menu, created by Maxim's, is the first class menu on Pan American's inaugural Boeing 707 flight from New York to Paris. *Martin Berinstein*

of introducing the 747, the company had lost $120 million. And then the price of jet fuel quadrupled as the Middle Eastern oil producers broke the western oil companies' monopoly on crude oil prices and formed a cartel of their own.

It was the beginning of the end for Pan American, although few could then imagine it. It did begin to regain its balance in the second half of the 1970s only to be felled by deregulation. It never had the financial resources to properly establish the national network that was crucial to its survival. The post-deregulation merger with National was too little too late.

Unable to generate the cash flow required to survive, Pan American lurched through the 1980s selling off its assets piecemeal to gain breathing space. Most humiliating was the sale to United of the historic, prestigious Pacific Division for a stunning $750 million. But in the end, none of it was enough. In November 1989, Pan American was grounded forever.

Its name and the blue-and-white globe that was its logo continue to fascinate. Entrepreneurs who bought the rights to them paint them on modest fleets of airplanes from time to time and bravely launch them into the fray. But these optimistic ventures are false echoes of Juan Trippe's Chosen Instrument. Its most fitting epitaph can occasionally be glimpsed on a bumper sticker popular with former employees and passengers who will forever love the world's greatest airline. It simply says in blue letters on a white background "Pan American. Gone but not forgotten."

Northwest

Byron Webster, a St. Paul, Minnesota, business-man, handed over $40 to become Northwest Airways' first fare-paying passenger on July 5, 1927. Bound for Chicago, 350 miles from his home-town as the crow flies, he wasn't quite sure what he was letting himself in for, but at least he knew he was in good hands. He was flying with Charles "Speed" Holman, Northwest's first pilot who was al-ready nationally famous for his air racing exploits.

They took off into changeable summer skies pro-tected from the elements by a novelty for their time, the enclosed cabin of Northwest's brand-new four-seat Stinson SB-1 Detroiter biplane. They flew via La Crosse, Madison, and Milwaukee, held up by an in-flight engine failure and weather along the way, and finally touched down in Chicago at 2:30 the follow-ing morning after a grueling 12.5 hours en route. Half a century later, a Northwest Boeing 747 would take as long to fly 6,000 miles nonstop from Min-neapolis/St. Paul to Tokyo, with room onboard for more than three times as many passengers as the en-tire airline carried in all of 1927.

Northwest was founded by Colonel Lewis Brit-tin with backing from Detroit businessmen—includ-ing Henry Ford—the year before Webster's flight with Speed Holman. Brittin was a West Point gradu-ate who worked for General Electric in Minneapolis. Bitten by the aviation bug when he served as an ar-tillery officer in World War I, he launched Northwest Airways with a successful bid on the air mail con-tract between the Twin Cities and Chicago.

Over the next five years Northwest expanded steadily in its region, extending its routes and build-ing a varied fleet to handle the growing volume of passengers and mail. A second route was opened to Chicago via Rochester, Minnesota, and a lakeshore route was established along Lake Michigan connect-ing Chicago with Green Bay, Wisconsin. To the north of the Twin Cities, service started to Fargo, North Dakota, and Northwest even went international by continuing on to Winnipeg, Canada. The Canadian government took a dim view of this brazen U.S. ex-pansion into its domain, and the Winnipeg service was temporarily shut down after only three months.

Northwest's fleet initially included four Stinson Detroiters for joint passenger and mail service, and a gaggle of Wacos, Lairds, and other types to carry mail exclusively. But by 1929 the need for larger aircraft was evident, and the company decided to acquire the latest equipment available. Through its Ford connec-tion, the selection of five 14-passenger Ford Trimo-tors was a natural choice. The Fords were joined by nine single-engined six-passenger Hamilton Met-alplanes. Although smaller than the Fords, they closely resembled them in construction and appear-ance, and cruised at approximately the same speed.

Of all the U.S. airlines that flew the Boeing 377 Stratocruiser, Northwest liked them the most. They served the airline's Far Eastern destinations and the prestigious Hawaii run. Northwest kept them in service longer than the other majors, and when the L-188 Electras were under severe speed restrictions because of the wing flutter problem, the airline briefly recalled its just phased-out Stratocruisers to help maintain its schedules.

The Lockheed Orion featured such advances as retractable gear, cantilever wing, and monocoque construction. It was one of the fastest aircraft of its time.

The Twin Cities area was a rather large population center by the late 1920s with strong commercial ties throughout the country. However, its remote northern location made it time consuming for travelers to link up overland with the nation's principal east-west rail network, and therein Northwest Airways saw an opportunity. Starting in 1928, the company introduced innovative air/rail services in cooperation with the railroads. Timetables were co-ordinated and Northwest began feeding a steady stream of passengers to the national railroad network's Chicago hub.

By the time Postmaster General Walter Folger Brown's spoils conferences got underway under the auspices of the Watres-McNary Act in 1930 to realign the airline industry, Northwest was in a good position to retain its air mail routes. Although it was one of the smaller carriers, it met all the criteria Brown was looking for in an airline he deemed suitable for carrying the mail. It had been in existence for half a decade, its fleet included modern multi-engined equipment, and it had substantial night flying experience.

Another advantage for Northwest was not having air mail contracts along the three transcontinental routes that Brown had earmarked for the three

strongest carriers at the expense of the weaker ones. So Northwest survived the spoils conferences intact and moved on to build its regional network. It also passed into the hands of a group of local businessmen, firmly planting its roots in Minneapolis/St. Paul for the long term.

In 1931 Northwest became an amphibian operator when it started serving Duluth, Minnesota, on the shore of Lake Superior. Duluth lacked a suitable airport but had a good harbor. Rather than delay service, the airline acquired two Sikorsky S-38s to fly the route for the two years it took to complete an airport.

The scope for further local expansion was limited, but from the beginning the airline's executives had been looking to the West's vast, open spaces for long-term growth opportunities, setting their sights as far as the Pacific coast. In the next two years, Northwest pushed its routes deep into Montana. By October 1933, it had reached Spokane, Washington, and on December 3, 1933, its first scheduled flight touched down in Seattle and Tacoma. Northwest had linked the Great Lakes and the Pacific, symbolically fulfilling the quest of the early explorers whose futile search for the Northwest Passage had inspired the airline's name.

Northwest was briefly an amphibian operator when it operated a Sikorsky S-38 to Duluth, Minnesota, on Lake Superior rather than wait two years for a suitable land airport to be built. Pan American operated 38 S-38s in South America and the Caribbean.

Northwest's ambitious new routes needed modern equipment, and an ambitious, up-and-coming aircraft manufacturer was eager to get the business. The company was Lockheed, and the first aircraft it sold Northwest were three swift, single-engined eight-seat Orion monoplanes. Their airframe was made of wood, but their advanced aerodynamic design, cantilever wing, and retractable gear pointed to the future. And the future was already on Lockheed's drawing board.

It was the L-10 Electra that incorporated all the major design advances then also being applied on the larger Douglas DC-2, which was initially too large for Northwest's needs. Northwest worked closely with Lockheed on the Electra's final specifications and took delivery of its first five aircraft in 1934 followed by another eight during the following year.

The year 1934 brought a crisis for Northwest, along with the rest of the airline industry, when the government gave the task of flying the air mail to the U.S. Army, nullifying the route allocations of the spoils conferences on grounds of bid rigging. But undermanned and untrained for airline flying, the Army quickly proved incapable of the job and after four months, the routes were re-awarded, mostly to the airlines that had held them. They had to change their names, however, and Northwest Airways became Northwest Airlines.

With one minor exception Northwest got back its old air mail routes, but its founder, Colonel Brittin, was needlessly claimed by the upheaval. He had done nothing wrong, but out of principle he refused to turn over personal papers to the congressional committee investigating the mail contracts and was convicted of contempt of Congress. Insulted, he resigned from Northwest, and spent his 10-day jail sentence as a house guest of the local sheriff.

When Northwest got back to business after the government-induced fiasco of 1934, the Electras proved a great success. But within two years, the growth in traffic and the quest for more performance justified further equipment expansion. Northwest's choice was the 14-passenger L-14 Super Electra, a scaled-up version of the L-10. Taking its cue from the railroad industry's practice of naming its flagship transcontinental express train services, Northwest named its L14 the Sky Zephyr and bought 11 of them over two years.

But the Sky Zephyrs weren't destined for long-term service. Traffic volume was increasing at such a pace that by the time they went on the line, they

Northwest's original logo prominently featured the air mail's central role in the airline's business. When after World War II it was replaced by a more modern stylized arrow motif the air mail reference was retained on the pilot's cap badge as a reminder of the past.

Northwest worked closely with Lockheed on the 10-seat L-10 Electra's final specifications, taking delivery of five aircraft in 1934 and a further eight the following year. The Electras were well suited for low-density feeder routes.

Northwest conducted pioneering research in adverse weather flying and high-altitude airline operations. Here a cabin load of Electra passengers don oxygen masks, which were used to safely cross the Rockies.

were obsolete. Northwest was ready for DC-3s and took delivery of the first one on April 22, 1939. By the end of 1940, all the Sky Zephyrs were gone, replaced by 13 DC-3s that were complemented on the lower-density routes by a reduced fleet of Electras.

This structure defined Northwest Airlines on the eve of World War II. It was a solid, midsized carrier with a challenging, far-flung route structure, and not the slightest inkling that the war would transform it into one of America's premiere international airlines.

By the time the war broke out, Northwest was one of America's most experienced bad weather and cold weather airlines. The climate along its routes across the Rockies into the Northwest was always unpredictable and treacherous, and the winter along its entire system was the most severe in the country. Its experience made the airline an ideal choice to set up a comprehensive contract Air Transport Command operation to various points in Alaska from the Midwest through Canada and later from Seattle.

Alaska was important because it was the main route for a massive flow of supplies and equipment to the Soviet Union to assist in its life-and-death struggle against Nazi Germany. It was also of strategic importance. Several Aleutian islands were the only American soil to be occupied by Japan.

Northwest's main Alaskan ports of call included Anchorage, Fairbanks, Fort Yukon, and Nome. Following the eviction of the Japanese from the Aleutians, the company set up service to Attu at the westernmost tip of the island chain, which grew to three daily roundtrips from Minneapolis at the height of the airlift. Aircraft used for the airlift were C-47s, C-46s, and the airline's own commandeered DC-3s. The Attu terminus was only 1,500 miles from Tokyo, less than the distance from Chicago to Seattle.

Northwest's Alaskan war effort was about twice the size of Western's similar operation. It also carried out important icing research during the war, and had 5,000 employees working on military aircraft completions at its Twin Cities home base. And when the war was over, it got its just rewards.

Its first postwar plum was in being made America's fourth transcontinental airline, cracking the long-standing monopoly held by United, TWA, and American. Northwest was approved to fly from the Twin Cities to New York via Milwaukee and Detroit, linking the Big Apple with Seattle on the nation's northernmost transcontinental route. This service was inaugurated by a DC-3 on June 1, 1945, when the war in the Pacific was still raging.

In 1946 service commenced to Anchorage from Seattle. From the following year, Northwest also began

NORTHWEST Orient AIRLINES

This early ticket jacket optimistically lists destinations in mainland China, to which Northwest won route awards. Shortly after the inaugural trips to the main destinations, the communist victory in China's civil war put on hold Northwest's ambitious Chinese plans for decades to come.

flying the so-called inside route to Alaska that it had pioneered during the war via Edmonton and Alberta, Canada.

Alaska itself was not the big prize, but a stepping stone to help Northwest achieve a much larger ambition. As soon as practical it intended to start flying to the Far East via Alaska with service to America's erstwhile archenemy, Japan, and on to Korea, China, and the Philippines. The Alaskan route to the Orient had an important advantage over the southern routes of rival Pan American. It was shorter by as much as 20 percent depending on destination. For East Coast travelers; it was the most direct route and had another advantage: It could be flown the entire way on one carrier.

But such an expanded long-range route system couldn't be served exclusively by an increasing number of war surplus DC-3s. It was once again time to acquire additional, more modern equipment. Like many of its peers, Northwest's immediate solution was the purchase of 18 Douglas DC-4s in late 1945 and 1946, 15 of which were C-54s reconditioned to civilian configuration. The DC-4s were well suited for the airline's route system and enjoyed a long service life. Eventually the DC-4 fleet numbered over 35 aircraft. Eleven were still in service in 1960 and the last ones weren't retired until the following year.

On July 15, 1947, Northwest passed a major milestone in its history with its inaugural service to the Far East. Three times a week, its DC-4s linked the Twin Cities with Tokyo, Seoul, Shanghai, and Manila via Anchorage and Shemya. The outbound trip to Tokyo took approximately 37 hours including the en route stops. The airline named its link to the Orient the Northwest Passage, a term used in its advertising throughout the 1950s. For the first time, it also began subtly referring to itself as Northwest Orient Airlines. Over time, the term appeared in advertising and in

Performance Progress

This table gives a summary taste of how airline performance increased over the years. Note how the fan-jet-powered B-747 manages to push range beyond the gas-guzzling first B-707. Most 707s were upgraded to fan-jets when they became available and gained another 1,000 miles in range.

Type and First Service	DC-3 (1936)	DC-6B (1951)	L-1649 (1957)	B-707 (1958)	B-747 (1970)
Cruise Speed (mph)	180	315	342	600	625
Range (sm)	500	3,000	5,280	3,000	5,800
Gross Weight (lbs)	25,200	107,000	156,000	248,000	713,000
Passengers	21	66	99	140	364

Source: R. E. G. Davies, *Airlines of the United States Since 1914.*

The DC-7 was an important addition to Northwest's fleet, successfully competing with the Lockheed Super Constellation. Its final variant, the stretched wing DC-7C, was the company's last piston liner. With its long range, it established one-stop Polar service from New York to Tokyo via Anchorage as the jet age loomed. Northwest's DC-7s remained with the airline as freighters for some time after the jets arrived.

discrete lettering on the nose of the aircraft. The name Northwest Orient, however, didn't appear in bold lettering on the fuselage until 1969 and the corporate name was never changed from Northwest Airlines.

Ambitious plans for service to cities throughout mainland China in the late 1940s were thwarted by the Communist victory in the civil war, which also forced Northwest to abandon Shanghai. Taipei replaced the mainland in the airline's itinerary. In short order Osaka, Okinawa, and Hong Kong (via a local feeder line) were also added to the schedule.

Closer to home, in the aftermath of World War II, Northwest joined its contemporaries in the quest for a replacement for the DC-3. Several airlines were considering both the Convair 240 and the Martin 202. Convair won a large order from American, and Martin was favored by Eastern. Northwest also opted for the 202 with an initial order of 10, subsequently increased to 25. When Eastern's order was delayed because of protracted wrangling about changes to the airplane, Northwest became its launch customer with what soon proved to be tragic results.

The first Martin 202s entered service in late 1947. Barely a year later, on August 26, 1948, a Northwest 202 with only 1,500 hours on it crashed in a thunderstorm near Winona, Minnesota, with no survivors. The first clue of structural failure was a wing found a long distance from the rest of the wreckage. The subsequent examination found that a poorly designed wing flange had failed well below the specified limit. Examination of Northwest's other 202s revealed serious cracks in the offending flange. The entire 202

fleet of 25 aircraft was grounded. A fix was subsequently found, but the grounding and three unrelated subsequent crashes of the type almost bankrupted the airline. Over the next two years the 202s were phased out, replaced by DC-3s and DC-4s (many of them hastily leased to deal with the problem) that they were to replace.

But all was not doom and gloom as the 1940s were coming to a close. The CAB's generous postwar mood continued unabated, bringing Northwest important additional domestic routes in 1948. The airline extended its reach toward the East with service to Cleveland, Pittsburgh, and Washington, D.C., a particularly useful addition in view of Northwest's oriental services used by U.S. government employees. But the year's big prize was another long western route, half way across the Pacific, from Seattle to Honolulu, Hawaii.

It was also the year when Northwest painted the entire tail of its aircraft in its trademark red, a feature that has since survived several paint scheme changes and lives on in the twenty-first century. It has been said that the red tail was adopted to provide a better chance of discovery in case of a forced landing somewhere along the airline's long, hostile routes, but this reason has never been officially acknowledged.

Following the Martin 202 fiasco, Northwest had much better luck with its next addition to the fleet, the majestic Boeing 377 Stratocruiser, ordered back in early 1946. A generation beyond the DC-4s, the luxurious, pressurized, 83-passenger Stratocruisers, with their overnight berths and famous downstairs bar, became Northwest's flagship airliners when they entered service in mid-1949. They served in that role in passengers' minds until the arrival of the jets in spite of later challenges from the faster Lockheed Super Constellations and the Douglas DC-7Cs.

Northwest's 10 Stratocruisers flew throughout the system, making a grand entrance on the Minneapolis–New York route closely followed by service to Seattle, Hawaii, and the Far East. While establishing new levels of passenger comfort, the Stratocruiser turned out to be maintenance intensive and not particularly profitable. Company wags used to joke that the Stratocruiser needed a 110 percent load factor to break even. Its massive engines were so prone to in-flight failure that it was nicknamed the best three-engined airliner across the oceans. But the passengers loved it, and to this day remember it with greater affection than any other propliner.

A year after the introduction of the Stratocruiser, the United States was once again embroiled in a distant war, this time on the Korean

This assembly of Northwest brochures from the 1940s and 1950s illustrates the airline's global reach. *Martin Berinstein*

peninsula. Northwest's employees had to temporarily flee Seoul under dramatic circumstances. But the war brought more business for the airline. With its well-established Far Eastern routes, it was the logical choice as prime contractor to provide air transport and cargo services under the Korean Airlift for the military.

The war's end saw another major expansion in equipment as the propliner era entered its final phase. Northwest's main acquisition was a fleet of pressurized DC-6s, the first of which were put on the line in late 1953. They were A models, leased from Flying Tiger, until Northwest's own DC-6Bs started arriving about two years later. In 1954 the company also placed orders for six Lockheed L-1049G Super Constellations for the Far Eastern routes.

The year 1954 brought an important change in the executive suite. Donald Nyrop took over as Northwest's new president and would lead the airline into the jet age and the brink of deregulation. Nyrop, who was the administrator of the CAB prior to joining Northwest, found the airline straining

under the financial burden of its fleet expansion and some mismatch of routes and equipment. Under his guidance, the airline restructured its financing, redistributed existing equipment, and adjusted its schedules. Nyrop also cancelled two of the Constellation orders, in part out of financial considerations, but also because he favored the airline's tradition of a standardized Douglas fleet. In line with this approach Northwest ordered its last piston airliner, the DC-7C, soon after Nyrop's arrival.

The 17 ultra-long-range Seven Seas that joined the Northwest fleet between 1957 and 1958 were perfect for the far-flung routes to the Orient, but the jets were already hot on their heels. As Northwest's last DC-7Cs joined the fleet, Pan American launched Boeing 707 jet service across the Atlantic and feisty National claimed first place in the domestic jet sweepstakes with two seasonally leased Pan American 707s.

As the propliners droned into the twilight of their golden age, the DC-7C made a pioneering contribution to Northwest's services. In the summer of

NORTHWEST *Orient* AIRLINES
"Aloha" Service

Hawaii was a big prize for Northwest. The airline started service to Honolulu from Seattle in 1948 and from California in 1969.

The quasi-military stewardess uniform that succeeded the nurse look in the 1930s endured into the swinging 1960s. It was replaced by a variety of riotously colorful, outlandish costumes at various airlines before a neutral, corporate look took hold in the 1980s.

1959 it inaugurated polar service to Tokyo from New York via Anchorage. Although soon superceded by the jets, Northwest's DC-7s got a new lease on life, serving as converted DC-7F freighters to the Far East until 1968, laying the foundations of a dedicated air freight division.

During the second half of the 1950s, Northwest's domestic expansion also continued. The most important new market was Florida, which the airline initially entered via an interchange agreement with Eastern on the Twin Cities–Chicago-Miami route in 1954. Northwest pilots flew the aircraft to Chicago, where Eastern's crews took over for the Miami leg. By 1958 the CAB authorized Northwest to provide its own service to the Southeast, and the interchange agreement was terminated. Another valuable route addition was service between Chicago and New York, which started in 1955.

Northwest's jets weren't long in coming as the airline industry experienced its most significant technological advance. The first turbine-powered airplane to join the airline's fleet was a 77-passenger turboprop that traced its roots back to its namesake, the airliner that had taken Northwest into the era of modern air transportation. It was the Lockheed L-188 Electra. It was a fine airliner, ideal for Northwest's medium-haul routes, but like the Martin 202 it had a fatal design flaw. And once again Northwest was to suffer the consequences.

On March 17, 1960, Northwest's first Electra, en route from Chicago to Miami, broke up in flight over Indiana for no apparent reason with the loss of all 68 passengers and crew. It was the second mysterious Electra crash, six months on the heels of a similar loss by Braniff. It would take nine months to establish that the culprit was an engine mount that induced wing flutter under the right circumstances. The Electras were restricted to piston propliner speed and had a tough time attracting passengers. Once a fix was found, they became highly reliable airplanes but were quickly eclipsed by the pure jets.

Northwest remained loyal to Douglas for the acquisition of its first pure jets, with an order for 10 DC-8s. But the transition wasn't entirely smooth. Production delays held up inauguration of Northwest's first DC-8 until July 1960, and by then five of the orders had been cancelled. Nevertheless, the DC-8

proved to be a stunning success on the Far Eastern routes, setting record flight times that were not exceeded until the commencement of nonstop crossings.

Northwest's extensive network of domestic medium-haul routes also made it a candidate for a jetliner with a shorter range than the DC-8. The airline chose the most viable alternative available at the time, the Boeing 720. It was a scaled-down, lighter version of the 707 with a substantially redesigned wing to better handle short field operations.

Welcome Aboard

This is your
SOUVENIR
FLIGHT BOOK
...yours to keep,
if you wish, with
our compliments

NORTHWEST *Orient* AIRLINES
St.Paul/Minneapolis, Minnesota
COAST TO COAST • FLORIDA • HAWAII
CANADA • ALASKA • THE ORIENT

Northwest's initial jet was the DC-8, introduced in July 1960. When production problems delayed delivery, the airline cut back its order from 10 to 5 and built up a big 707 fleet that had some commonality with the Boeing 720s ordered in the meantime.

Concurrent with its Boeing 720 selection, Northwest began negotiations for acquiring the Boeing 707-320 Intercontinental for its long-range international routes. It was the beginning of a close long-term relationship with Boeing to the disadvantage of Douglas. The first of 17 Boeing 720s was delivered to Northwest in mid-1961. They were introduced on the Twin Cities–Chicago–New York route, and by late 1962, they ranged from New York all the way to Hawaii via the Pacific Northwest.

The 707-320 made its debut two years later, and soon thereafter the five DC-8s were sold. The total number of 707s in Northwest's fleet ultimately reached 36 with deliveries taking place as late as 1968.

By the time Northwest's Boeing 720s began appearing on the airways, the design destined to be one of the most successful medium-range airliners ever built was on the drawing board. It was the Boeing 727, the three-holer, and it would become the most numerous airplane in Northwest's fleet. Although not a launch customer for the 727, Northwest wasn't far behind, taking delivery of its first three 727-100s in 1964. A year later they were followed by the first 727-200s, which carried 10 more passengers than the 720s and were more economical to run.

The massive aircraft acquisition program was merely keeping pace with the expansion in services.

Northwest's Lockheed L-188 Electras provided excellent service on medium-haul routes for about a decade, in spite of the company's bad luck with the type when it was introduced. Northwest suffered one of the two fatal accidents due to structural failure that put the Electra's future in doubt for over a year.

Northwest enthusiastically embraced the Boeing 727-100, putting the first three into service in 1964. Eventually the 727 became the most numerous aircraft in Northwest's fleet.

The frequency of service was increased within the system, more direct flights were offered between an increasing number of city pairs, and additional routes were acquired. Northwest was finally allowed into Southern California and was also given the coveted right to serve Hawaii from there. In late 1969 it introduced Los Angeles–Honolulu-Tokyo service, closing the circle around the Pacific. And Northwest made its first foray into Europe with a through-plane interchange agreement with Pan American, opening what it called the Northeast Passage from the Twin Cities to London-Heathrow via New York.

The same year saw the dawn of the widebody era when Pan American inaugurated Boeing 747 service between New York and London. Like most of its peers, Northwest jumped on the Jumbo Jet bandwagon, but unlike several of them it had the long-range routes to support the jets. Boeing 747 service commenced in June 1970, and by the end of the fol-

lowing year, 15 of the giant jetliners were roaming the Pacific in Northwest colors from as far away as New York.

Northwest also recognized the need for a wide-body smaller than the Boeing 747 and returned to Douglas for a solution, selecting the DC-10 with an interesting twist. It ordered the airplane with improvements that gave it intercontinental range and engine commonality with the airline's Boeing 747s, yielding great economies of scale in engine maintenance. To achieve the required performance, the DC-10's wingspan had to be slightly extended and fuel capacity had to be increased. To support the attendant increase in weight, it required a third main landing gear. This version was the DC-10-40 and it entered service in late 1972 between the Twin Cities and Tampa, Florida. Within three years, the DC-10 fleet had risen to 22 and was in widespread use on high-density domestic and international routes.

Northwest takes delivery of the 707th 707, commemorated in a Boeing photo. Note the racy stewardess outfits that had replaced the classic quasi-military uniform look.

With its far-flung Far East routes, Northwest was an important Boeing 747 customer, flying 15 of the behemoths by the end of 1971. The 747s proved to be a real Pacific workhorse along with the smaller DC-10s. Northwest also became a freight 747 operator. This passenger version is seen ferrying a spare engine on the port inboard pylon.

By the time the oil crisis of the 1970s hit, Northwest was in a better position than some of its peers to weather the storm. Don Nyrop's tough fiscal management had made it one of the most profitable U.S. airlines, and its Far Eastern routes stood to benefit handsomely from Asia's coming economic ascendance.

Deregulation would bring massive expansion, in large part through the acquisition of such large regionals as Republic Airlines and Hughes Airwest. It would open routes to Europe and new destinations in the Far East. It would also bring a period of intense financial hardship and doubts about the future. But Northwest would fight back with the same tenacity that drove it to reach the West Coast with its Ford Trimotors, and to open the forbidding Alaskan route to the Far East in propliner days. And it would ultimately face the twenty-first century with the same high level of optimism that enabled it to cajole Byron Webster out of $40 to become its first passenger back when the only way across the oceans was by boat.

Delta

Had the U.S. Department of Agriculture not sent two entomologists to Louisiana to declare war on the boll weevil, there may never have been a Delta Airlines. The two scientists, B. R. Coad and C. E. Woolman, identified the pesticides that most effectively zapped the tiny insect with a voracious appetite for the annual cotton crop and chose a novel high-tech approach to dispense it. They loaded the poisonous powder in a hopper onboard a Huff Daland Petrel biplane modified for the purpose, and dusted the unsuspecting pests from on high.

The experiments founded the crop dusting profession, but they also made another contribution to the future of the aviation industry. They so hooked C. E. Woolman on the possibilities of flight that he went on to establish Delta Airlines and lead it over three and a half decades into the jet age.

First came Huff Daland Dusters, set up with the majority control of Huff Daland Airplanes in 1924 to treat the deep South's cotton crop. Established in Macon, Georgia, and Monroe, Louisiana, it signed on C. E. Woolman as its chief entomologist. The company did well, but the business was seasonal, so, like many duster operators to come, it decided to follow the seasons to find work throughout the year. By the 1926 U.S. off-season, it was established in Lima, Peru, with five dusters to treat the local cotton crop.

Realizing the potential for air travel in the vast mountainous country where mule trains were still the norm, in 1928 Huff Daland Dusters acquired an air mail and passenger service certificate from the Peruvian authorities. The certificate attracted the attention of Juan Trippe and his associates, eager to spread Pan American's wings throughout South America, and the two parties made a deal. Trippe provided a Fairchild FC-2 to launch Peruvian Airways, and leased Huff Daland's certificate to operate it. When Pan American and W. R. Grace and Company formed Pan American Grace Airways to serve the western half of South America, the new venture swallowed Peruvian Airways.

Eager to capitalize on his Peruvian adventures, C. E. Woolman headed north and bought out Huff Daland with backing from the Monroe, Louisiana, business community. The war on bugs continued, but plans were also laid for passenger service between Dallas, Texas, and Jackson, Mississippi, via Shreveport and Monroe, Louisiana. To reflect its geographic association with the fertile, flat expanse where the Mississippi River flows into the Gulf of Mexico, it was named Delta Air Service.

On June 17, 1929, Delta inaugurated passenger service with one of two newly acquired Travel Air 6000s. In September 1929 Delta extended its route to

Delta scooped Eastern with jet service when Eastern decided to wait for a more powerful version of the DC-8 and gave up its early delivery positions. Delta promptly grabbed them and was first with the DC-8 on September 18, 1959, placing it in service between New York and Atlanta and beating United into the air by three hours. The DC-8 was about a year behind the introduction of the Boeing 707.

One of the Huff Daland dusters that started it all. C. E. Woolman, Delta's founder and long-time CEO, was an entomologist who played a key role in developing aerial crop spraying. He was so inspired by his brush with aviation that he went on to create Delta Airlines. Delta's crop spraying division survived into the 1970s.

Fort Worth, Texas, to the west and Birmingham, Alabama, to the east. The following year it intended to push on to Atlanta, Georgia, to link up with Eastern Air Lines' north-south mail network. Eastern was to obtain an Atlanta–New Orleans mail route, which Delta would operate for it. But these well-laid plans were thwarted by the Watres-McNary Act and Postmaster General Walter Folger Brown.

With no large aircraft, no night flying experience, and less than two years of operations, Delta was considered so unqualified that it wasn't even invited to attend the spoils conferences that redrew the nation's air mail map. The mail contracts it had hoped to get were awarded to American Airways, and Delta was back to crop dusting exclusively.

But the allure of flying passengers remained strong, and within four years, in a striking reversal of fortune C. E. Woolman and his company were back in the airline business.

Delta's salvation was the 1934 Air Mail Act that redistributed the 1930 spoils conferences air mail route allocations after charges of bid rigging and a four-month interlude when the U.S. Army's fliers carried the mail with disastrous results. Most routes were returned to its previous holders operating under new names, but a few new winners emerged, Delta among them. The route it won included its

original nonsubsidized route and pushed it on to Atlanta and beyond to Charleston, South Carolina.

Delta hastily acquired six Stinson 6000B Trimotors from American Airways and launched the first mail flight from Dallas on July 4, 1934. Passenger service followed a month later.

Delta needed more capital to grow, and it was forthcoming from banker and publisher, Clarence Faulk, another Monroe, Louisiana, businessman, who bought a controlling interest in the rejuvenated company. Faulk remained a staunch supporter, serving as Delta's chairman from 1945 until his death six years later.

Faulk's capital bought two Stinson Model As, low-wing trimotors designed to supercede the 6000Bs. The Model As were not the most stable aircraft, but they were faster than their predecessors and more luxurious. To add a bit of railroad-inspired style, westbound Model A service was *The Texan*, eastbound, *The Georgian*.

Late that year Delta introduced the Lockheed 10 Electra. A fast all-metal retractable gear twin, the 10-seat Electra had all the state-of-the-art attributes of the larger DC-2, and DC-3, complementing them on lower-density routes.

The Dallas-Atlanta segment, however, generated enough peak demand to justify acquiring the Queen

A rare photo of a Chicago and Southern Stinson Trimotor, the type also flown by Delta briefly, starting in 1934. Chicago and Southern was a Midwestern regional airline that extended its reach all the way down to New Orleans, and after World War II was authorized to go on to Caracas, Venezuela, and Havana, Cuba. It merged with Delta in 1953, doubling the combined airlines' route system.

of the Art Deco skies, the DC-3. But there was a long waiting list for DC-3s as the larger airlines replaced the DC-2s. Delta thus purchased four ex-American Airlines DC-2s in early 1940 as an interim solution, replacing them by year's end with five DC-3s.

In March 1941, Delta recognized an inevitable consequence of its growth and moved its headquarters to Atlanta, which was bigger and more centrally located on its system than Monroe. But it remained loyal to its Mississippi Delta roots, holding its annual meetings in Monroe long into the jet age.

Within two months came a pivotal route award, initiating the foundations of national expansion. Delta was authorized to provide service from Atlanta to Cincinnati, Ohio, tantalizingly close to Chicago. It also got a spur down south to Savannah, Georgia.

But World War II put all plans on hold as Delta made its own contribution to the war effort along with its contemporaries. Most of Delta's wartime service was within the United States, flying cargo and providing medical flights to disperse incoming war-wounded among the nation's hospitals. The company also operated important modification and completion centers, making, among other mods, the long-range fuel tanks that enabled P-51 Mustangs to escort allied bombers deep into Germany.

Delta's most unusual contribution to the war was a fleet of giant Bug Killers. They were C-47s converted to crop dusters by the airline's dusting division that was still doing a booming business long after it was dwarfed by the airline operations. Delta pilots flew them on pest control missions, mostly over mosquito infested islands in the Pacific.

As the war wound down, the CAB was well disposed toward fostering competition among the airlines, and Delta was a major beneficiary. An early appetizer was a route award branching off from the Dallas-Atlanta route to New Orleans. The awards that followed kicked off Delta's transformation over time from a regional, mostly southern carrier into a national airline.

In the summer of 1945, as Japan was about to fall, the CAB presented Delta with a personal victory prize, granting it the Atlanta-Miami route via Jacksonville. Then came a Christmas present extending the Cincinnati terminus up to Chicago. All of a sudden the company that little over a decade before seemed destined to bash bugs for the rest of its days was a major airline, counting among its destinations the population centers of Chicago, Atlanta, Miami, Dallas, and New Orleans.

The CAB's benevolence was prompted by the monopoly Eastern Airlines had throughout the region before the war. While the other three members of the so-called Big Four competed in a fashion across the continent, Eastern had been unchallenged in the East. Another airline that benefited from the CAB's new outlook was National, which was granted the New York–Miami route in competition with Eastern immediately after the war.

Delta proudly displayed the DC-3 on its baggage tags once it got its first DC-3s at the end of 1940. Although a regional, Delta had several large population centers in its network that justified the airplane.

To handle such an increase in its network, Delta needed a major expansion of its fleet, and Uncle Sam had just what it was looking for. First, the government released eight DC-3s to the airline, followed by a steady stream of surplus C-54s that Douglas was converting to airline configuration as quickly as it could.

December 1, 1945, was a landmark day for Delta, when a DC-3 inaugurated the Chicago-Miami route. It was a milk run with six stops along the way, but a lucrative one. And by February 1946 the airline received the first of its DC-4s. Within a month, DC-4 *Rocket* service opened on the route and within a year, the DC-4s launched the first ever nonstop service between the Windy City and the Sunshine State.

Eastern Airlines countered this audacious invasion of its jealously guarded turf by putting its Lockheed 649 Constellations on the route. The fast, pressurized, high fliers were soon leaving the DC-4s in their propwash, decimating Delta's load factors.

The intense Lockheed-Douglas competition to build the best piston liner in the world got underway in earnest and would run for a decade. Delta remained loyal to Douglas, responding to the Connies of the Great Silver Fleet by ordering in early 1948 Long Beach's somewhat belated reaction to the racy propliner from Burbank, the pressurized DC-6. Delta's coming DC-6s were advertised "300 Plus-Deltaliners" and much was made of the plush Sky Lounge for six in the rear. When they entered service toward the end of the year they proved to be faster than Eastern's Constellations, recapturing a fair share of the market.

By the end of the 1940s, Delta was one of several major airlines that sensed the potential benefit of providing service beyond their authorized routes without their passengers having to change aircraft. They got around their route restrictions by collaborating with each other with the CAB's approval.

Many airlines flew Curtiss C-46 cargo planes during World War II for the military under their contracts with Air Transport Command. Less known is that several airlines, including Delta, acquired surplus C-46's after the war and flew them as freighters. It was well suited for the role with a cargo capacity exceeding the DC-3's capacity by almost a third.
Lawrence Feir

The pressurized Convair 340 was Delta's choice to replace not only the DC-3 but also the DC-4 on short- and medium-haul routes. The CV 340 was introduced in 1952 and within the next two years, 20 of them joined Delta's fleet. The Delta C&S designation was used for two years after the merger with Chicago and Southern to retain C&S passenger loyalty and its important contribution to Delta.

The mechanism was the interchange agreement similar to the one United and Western had before the war on their joint DST sleeper service between Chicago and Los Angeles via Salt Lake City. The participants of an interchange agreement used the same aircraft for an entire flight, with flight crews from each airline taking turns to fly the aircraft through their own territory.

Delta participated in several interchange agreements starting in 1949 and reaching their peak during the 1950s. The most elaborate one was a three-way interchange with National and American, which got Delta all the way out to California. The route ran from Miami to San Francisco via New Orleans and Dallas. A National crew flew the airplane to New Orleans, a Delta crew took it on to Dallas, and an American crew flew it out to San Francisco. Depending on scheduling, the airplane could come from the fleet of any of the participating airlines.

Interchange services were popular with passengers who didn't have to worry about missing connections on a long journey. Airlines liked them because they made it possible to show the company colors in markets otherwise off limits. The exposure gained was seen as having potentially helpful influence on justifying future route applications.

As the postwar era got underway, Delta, like its contemporaries, had to consider a replacement for the DC-3. The company flirted with the unpressurized Martin 202, going as far as taking an option for

10 aircraft in mid-1946. A year later, Delta had a chance to put a prototype through its paces and found it wanting. Tragically, at about the same time, eight senior executives of the airline perished in a midair collision between the DC-3 they were flying and a private aircraft. As a result of these two events, the 202 options were not exercised and a decision on the DC-3's successor was temporarily put on hold.

Rejecting the Martin 202 may have increased the competitive pressure on Delta, but the missed opportunity had a silver lining. The airline escaped the potential disaster lurking in the 202's fatally flawed wing design.

Delta took some time making its next choice, passing up both the improved 202, which became the highly successful Martin 404, and the Convair 240. It eventually selected the upgraded version of the Convair 240, the more powerful, stretched CV 340, placing an initial order of 10 aircraft in 1951. The first CV 340s went into service at the end of 1952 and within the next two years, Delta was operating 20 of the versatile short-haul propliners. In 1956 and 1957, the company acquired eight Convair 440s, featuring an increase in gross weight and lowered cabin noise levels. Concurrently the 340 fleet was upgraded to the 440s specifications. But the diminishing fleet of DC-3s soldiered on, the last one not retiring until 1960 from an Owl night coach run.

During 1953, another pivotal year in Delta's history, the Airline of the South expanded its reach in

the eastern United States by half and became an international airline serving select Caribbean destinations. It accomplished this expansion not by internal growth, but by merging with Chicago and Southern (C&S), a vibrant but now largely forgotten airline.

Chicago and Southern, like Delta, got its break in the 1934 reallocation of the air mail routes, when it made the winning bid on the Chicago–New Orleans route via St. Louis and Memphis. Like Delta it built its business with Stinson Trimotors, replaced by Lockheed 10 Electras and a fleet of DC-3s. Its destinations expanded to include Kansas City, Houston, and Detroit.

Following World War II, C&S won a route extension from New Orleans to Caracas, Venezuela, via Havana, Cuba, and a branch from Havana to San Juan. With the war's end came five DC-4s and starting in 1950 the airline's flagship fleet of six Lockheed 649A Constellations.

The merger was a tremendous boost to Delta, which, out of deference to its substantial partner and to retain the loyalty of the acquired customer base, agreed to be called Delta–C&S for two years before reverting to its old name. The C&S Connies were quickly phased out to maintain an all-Douglas fleet, but Delta wasn't finished with the Constellation yet.

In the meantime, Eastern had countered the DC-6 with a fleet of Super Constellations, to which Delta responded with the turbo-compound engine-equipped DC-7 in 1954. An eight-seat Sky Room and a six-seat Sky Lounge enticed passengers on board Delta's DC-7 Gold Crown service in addition to the two-section main cabin.

As Delta built experience with the DC-7s, it got another long-coveted boost to its system. On January 20, 1956, the CAB authorized it to fly into New York.

The DC-7 joined Delta's fleet in 1954. In early 1956 it launched all first class service between New York and Atlanta when Delta was awarded the route, complemented by all coach DC-6 service. Subsequently the DC-7's also flew in mixed class configuration throughout Delta's system.

The Universal Air Travel Plan was an industrywide scheme first introduced in the late 1930s to allow holders of Air Travel Cards to charge tickets against prepaid deposits. The tickets bought under the air travel plan were discounted to encourage participation. Many corporations deposited a large ticket fund with an airline and then had the airline issue air travel cards to designated employees.

Ten days later, DC-6 coach service and DC-7 first class service was launched between the Big Apple and Atlanta. The award also extended to points in between, adding such population centers as Philadelphia, Baltimore, and Washington, D.C., to Delta's system. The increase in demand was so great that Delta bought four ex-Pan American 049 Constellations to help handle the load until more DC-7s came on line.

Delta's last propliner to join the fleet was the DC-7B, featuring Royal Crown service to keep the competition at bay on the increasingly common route segments. An extra flight attendant, increased beverage service, a choice of sumptuous entrées that reached beyond the traditional beef or chicken, free champagne, and taped music coddled Royal Crown passengers aloft. Expedited baggage service and dedicated reception agents smoothed the passengers' way on the ground. But by the time the first of the DC-7Bs joined the fleet, preparations were in the advanced stage to launch Delta into the jet age.

Perceptively, Delta decided to forego the interim turboprop step on the way to pure jets. Less perceptively, it was somewhat behind its contemporaries in making a type decision. Consequently it was facing a 1962 delivery date for its first DC-8s, risking a serious competitive disadvantage against Eastern and National, both of whom preceded Delta in the DC-8 line. But in the eleventh hour, salvation was at hand in the person of none other than Captain Eddie Rickenbacker.

Eastern's conservative president was all set to launch DC-8 service in 1959, but the captain always cared more about getting the most for his money than being first. Learning that the jet was soon to be available with the more powerful fan-jet engine that wouldn't require water injection to stagger into the air, he shocked his airline by promptly canceling Eastern's first six DC-8s that had the earlier engines. Delta grabbed them.

And so, on September 18, 1959, Delta became the first airline to operate the DC-8 in scheduled service with a nonstop flight from New York to Atlanta, which beat the first scheduled United DC-8 into the air by a few hours.

Delta's DC-8 proved wildly popular throughout the system, water-injected engines notwithstanding. Captain Eddie was soon forced to contemplate the wisdom of his ways when they took so much traffic away from Eastern's brand-new turboprop Lockheed Electras that he had to temporarily suspend service on competing routes until his own DC-8s arrived.

While the DC-8 and the Boeing 707 thrilled the traveling public, they were primarily long-range jets,

designed for the transcontinental and international routes. Airlines like Delta were keen to have a shorter-range option with fewer seats and better suited for their route system. Boeing developed the 720, but for Delta the preferred choice was the 84-seat Convair 880. It was to be the fastest jet made, and was instigated primarily by TWA, which intended to use it on premium all-first-class transcontinental dashes as well as medium-range flights.

Because TWA was experiencing financial problems, Delta's Convairs were the first into service in mid-1960, and within two years the fleet size grew to 17. As promised, they were the fastest jet transports, cruising at 568 miles per hour, but were not as successful as expected because of excessive fuel consumption. Flying them fast reduced their reach on longer flights, thwarting TWA's transcontinental plans. But they were a better match for Delta's route system and faithfully served the airline for 14 years.

As it entered the jet age, Delta accomplished other important milestones in its relentless quest to grow. In the spring of 1961, it became a transcontinental airline, approved to serve California from the Southeast. It was also authorized to provide through-service from California to the Caribbean. And two years later, it got its first taste of access to Europe with an interchange agreement with Pan American that provided DC-8 through-service from

The DC-7 is advertised on the back of this postcard as providing a Velvet Ride, cruising at 365 miles per hour at 25,000 feet, and providing first class Royal Crown service featuring complimentary champagne, a choice of several entrees, continuous beverage service, taped music, an extra stewardess, and expedited baggage handling.

Where DELTA serves
Domestic route mileage 10,849 — Foreign route mileage 3,239 — Total mileage 14,088

Total passengers carried to
Dec. 31, 1961 32,500,000
Revenue Passenger Miles

By 1961 Delta realized its long-standing ambition of serving the West Coast from its southern stronghold. Initial service was via interim stops, but direct flights from Atlanta and elsewhere soon followed. The western routes made Delta a truly national airline. The gaping white space on the map to the northwest would be filled in 1987, long after deregulation, by the acquisition of Western.

New Orleans and Atlanta to London and other points in Europe via Washington, D.C.

In the meantime, Delta continued to seek a truly short-haul jet that would fly Convair 340 stage lengths equally economically. The European manufacturers had the lead in this segment and several U.S. airlines turned to them for answers. United flew Sud Aviation Caravelles and Braniff and American Airlines opted for BAC 111s. Delta consulted Douglas, which had seriously considered license manufacturing the

Delta was the first customer for the DC-9, the short range jet the airlines had waited over five years to put in service.

Caravelle, and the result was one of the most successful short-haul airliners, the DC-9.

Delta initially ordered 15 DC-9-14s, which were restricted to a gross weight of 84,000 pounds to qualify for being flown with a two-person crew. But Douglas had designed the DC-9 with major expansion in mind and as soon as the weight restriction was eased by the FAA, the company introduced the stretched series 30. Delta launched DC-9-14 service in December 1965, followed by the introduction of the larger series 30 two years later, soon after Eastern Airlines launched the type. By the early 1970s, Delta's DC-9-32 fleet numbered 63 and went on to serve for the next two decades.

In 1968 Delta put in service the most audacious Douglas rubber band derivative, the stretched DC-8-61, to serve its high-density long-haul routes. The Super DC-8 increased passenger capacity by a remarkable 60 percent with an attendant increase in operating costs of only about 10 percent. It was an outstanding achievement, raising the upper passenger limit of narrowbody jets to 252. But it was about to be upstaged by the ultimate twentieth-century airliner, the jumbo jet, and Delta had no intention of being left out.

The Boeing 747 that Juan Trippe foisted on the world was an airplane few domestic airlines needed but none could afford to be without. Although it was too large even for transcontinental service in view of passenger volumes and fluctuations, the herd mentality took hold; afraid of being left behind, nine U.S. trunk lines ordered the magnificent beast in the mid-1960s. In October 1970, Delta inaugurated 747 service with a flight from Atlanta to Los Angeles via Dallas. But the company bought only five 747s, focusing on the smaller widebodies in the 250-seat range that were more suitable for its routes and was on its way.

Delta broke with tradition when it selected its next widebody, bypassing the Douglas DC-10 for the Lockheed L-1011 with an order for 24 aircraft. However, when the L-1011 program experienced delays because its engine supplier, Rolls-Royce, temporarily went into protective receivership, Delta hedged its bets by ordering five DC-10s to alleviate any delays in L-1011 deliveries. As a result, Delta became the first airline to operate all three widebody types simultaneously. By 1975, the DC-10s were gone and Delta went on to operate as many as 53 L-1011s.

In 1972 Delta achieved another long-sought addition to its route network by gaining access to New England when it completed the acquisition of Northeast Airlines. Technically considered a trunk line, this Boston-based carrier was another colorful regional airline with roots reaching all the way back to the 1930s and strong ambitions to expand beyond its home turf. After playing a pioneering role in opening up the North Atlantic routes during World War II, Northeast was allowed to expand to New York City and Montreal by the CAB, but was frustrated in growing further until 1956, when it received access to the increasingly lucrative Miami market.

From the late 1950s and 1960s, Northeast expanded aggressively, putting into service the Vickers Viscount and no less than four models of jetliners, the DC-9, B-727, CV 880, and CV 990. But it never had the long-haul routes to support its ambitions and lurched from financial crisis to crisis. A merger with Northwest was aborted in the last minute, and the only remaining option to the Delta merger was bankruptcy.

Delta retained Northeast's 727-200s and was by then expecting the first of its own three-holers. Although the airline was late in selecting the 727, it

This brochure features Delta's Douglas DC-9, Boeing 727, and Lockheed L-1011, representing all three manufacturers that provided jets for the airline, and distinguishing between the short-, medium-, and widebody long-haul use.

eventually built up a fleet of 727s, becoming the biggest operator of the type.

Northeast's system was a welcome addition to Delta's network, placing the airline's coverage and level of service in league with the industry leaders. Slowly, but surely the Big Four was becoming the Big Five. Delta's long track record of outstanding management saw it through the crises of the 1970s and the trauma of deregulation that followed. During the 1980s, its international operations grew substantially, particularly to Europe, and in 1989, it became America's fourth largest airline when it joined forces with Western in one of the most logical mergers in the industry. And at the Delta Air Museum in Atlanta, visitors can still see the Huff Daland crop duster that started it all.

CHAPTER 9

Continental

When United Airlines acquired Varney Air Lines in 1930, its restless founder, Walter Varney didn't lie back to savor the narrow escape he had from his creditors. He whipped into existence a succession of small airlines in the Southwest and quickly abandoned them when they failed to live up to his great plans. By 1934 he had moved beyond his fifth struggling venture, Varney Speed Lines, Southern Division, leaving it in the hands of Louis Muller, his World War I Army flight instructor.

Varney Speed Lines, renamed Varney Air Transport, had four Lockheed Vegas, the Pueblo–El Paso air mail route accompanied by a passengers-only segment between Denver and Pueblo, and a chronic shortage of cash. It attracted the attention of Robert F. Six, a brash young Californian pilot itching to run an airline of his own. For $90,000, which he charmed out of the skeptical chairman of the Pfizer Drug Company, who also happened to be his father-in-law, Robert Six bought 40 percent of Varney Air Transport in 1936. Two years later, he was elected president and easily convinced Muller that to reflect their ambitions they should rename their venture Continental Airlines.

Six was a relative latecomer to the airline game, but he would go on to run Continental for almost four decades, transforming it from its obscure begin-

nings into one of America's best-managed and most consistently profitable national airlines.

Along with the new name, Continental acquired a new logo featuring an Indian head motif, reflecting Six's deep fascination with western lore. The new chief's immediate priority upon taking the helm was to get bigger aircraft to better serve the modestly growing airline. Continental had acquired the air mail rights on the Denver-Pueblo route from a rival, and passenger demand was also up. The airline's north-south milk run didn't look like much of a route at face value, but it fed nicely into the growing national air transport system, connecting with the transcontinental routes of United at Denver, TWA at Albuquerque, and American at El Paso.

Soon after Six joined the company, he helped it acquire three six-passenger Lockheed L-12 Junior Electras. They took Continental into the modern airliner era and met the new twin-engine requirement for airlines to carry passengers, but were too small to provide more than an interim solution. Continental stepped up to the 10-passenger L-14 Super Electra in 1938, followed two years later by the Lockheed L-18 Lodestar. On the eve of World War II, it flew an all-Lodestar fleet of six aircraft and had expanded service as far as Wichita, Kansas, and Carlsbad, New Mexico. With the Lodestars came Continental's first flight attendants.

Continental put in service its first DC-3s as World War II was coming to an end. Within 15 years it would be flying Boeing 707s. The eagle logo replaced Continental's original Indian head motif when the DC-3 was introduced.
Lawrence Feir

During the war, the airline surrendered three of its Lodestars to serve Air Transport Command and ran a bomber modification center at its Denver base. Many of its employees, led by their president, joined the armed forces. Six served at various ferry bases, flying B-17s and B-24s among other types, roaming as far as Brazil and Australia. Ironically, the greatest wartime threat to his future came not from the enemy in some far off land but from a palace coup mounted by the ambitious, young executive he had put in temporary charge of Continental.

The caretaker Six chose, Terrence Drinkwater, did such an outstanding job and so enjoyed his new responsibilities that he tried to make them permanent. He engineered a board meeting to oust Six in his absence and had a strong chance of succeeding—until Robert Six himself strolled into the meeting. Secretly alerted by loyal supporters, he rode to his own rescue and squashed the revolt. Drinkwater shortly left Continental for a brief stint at American Airlines and then realized his ambitions at Western, which he ran with great skill and style for many years.

With its chief firmly back in the saddle as the war was coming to an end, Continental prepared for the expected postwar boom by putting in service the first of 12 DC-3s and exchanging the regional Indian head

Continental put five 44-seat, pressurized Convair 240s in service at the end of 1948. They were exceptionally well suited for the airline's high-altitude Rocky Mountain destinations. Later Continental also operated Convair 340s and 440s.

Continental's Convair liners plied the Blue Skyway, serving some of the most picturesque wilderness destinations in the West, which was attracting growing numbers of increasingly affluent visitors during the 1950s.

The British Vickers Viscount's reliable Rolls Royce turboprops gave a smooth jet ride 100 miles per hour faster than the DC-7's pounding pistons. Continental flew a fleet of 15 Viscount turboprops, the first of which were delivered in 1958. They flew in all-first class configuration between Los Angeles, Denver, and Chicago. The Viscount's gave Continental the biggest share in these markets competing with the DC-7 for about a year until the larger turboprop Lockheed Electras and pure jet 707s pushed them out.

1958

CONTINENTAL AIRLINES

VICKERS-VISCOUNT JET-PROP AIRLINER

motif for America's more enduring national symbol, a stylized eagle. The airline also got back its war veteran Lodestars, but as more DC-3s joined the fleet they were phased out. The DC-3s, however, were themselves soon to be relegated to secondary importance, because even as they were being introduced, Continental was looking at the 40+ passenger Martin 202 and the Convair 240.

The company chose the pressurized Convair 240, ordering five and putting them in service in December 1948. They featured unusual right-side air stair doors and were promoted as flying their passengers on The Blue Skyway. To better control service quality, with the arrival of the CV 240s Continental also established its own flight kitchen, modeled on United's pioneering experience.

In spite of these developments, in the immediate postwar years the expected boom didn't materialize, and Continental was stagnating because it couldn't get new route awards. That it managed to be marginally profitable throughout these lean years is testimonial to Six's business skills. He was famous for roaming the line unannounced and losing his temper at the smallest errors for which he saw no excuse. He also showed great compassion for mistakes that weren't an employee's fault and inspired remarkable staff loyalty. However, to warn their colleagues of an imminent Six inspection, his underlings devised a novel system that predated World War II. If they knew he was on the way, they'd call the station on the radio and say "Radio check, one, two, three, four, five, SIX!"

Continental peeked beyond its restricted route structure for the first time as the 1940s drew to a close by entering into a through-plane interline agreement with American and Braniff on the Houston–Los Angeles route, operated with DC-6Bs. Braniff crews flew the airplane from Houston to San Antonio; Continental flew the San Antonio–El Paso leg; and American operated the El Paso–Los Angeles segment. Shortly after service started in 1951, Braniff withdrew, giving Continental the Houston–San Antonio leg with the CAB's approval.

Business was sufficiently good that year to prompt Six to order seven Convair 340s, the stretched, more powerful replacement for the CV 240s. He also committed the airline for the first time to flying four-engined equipment with an order for two 58-seat DC-6Bs.

Continental's first significant postwar regional route expansion came with the acquisition of Pioneer Airlines in 1953, a local service carrier that flew to 22 destinations in Texas and New Mexico. Pioneer had upgraded its DC-3 fleet to nine ex-Northwest Martin 202s, but the CAB didn't authorize additional subsidies to offset the more expensive operating costs, and Pioneer was forced to sell out. The big prize in the package for Continental was access to Dallas, Austin, and increased access to Houston. The acquisition also brought to Continental Harding Lawrence, who would become Bob Six's understudy and would go on to lead Braniff on one of the wildest rides in air transport history.

The company didn't keep any Martin 202s beyond the merger transition. To handle the increased equipment demands, it squeezed out more work from its Convair fleet and beefed it up with three new Convair 440s.

Continental's big break came at last in November 1955. Six had taken every opportunity to file for a wide range of route applications over the years to no avail. Now, quite unexpectedly, the CAB granted Continental rights between Chicago and Los Angeles not only via Kansas City and Denver but also nonstop, a right the airline hadn't even requested. The Continental community was ecstatic. Here was the chance to become a national airline, to take on TWA, United, and American; and Bob Six wasn't about to blow it.

To equip Continental for the challenges of the exciting new route awards, Six devised a three-pronged strategy and launched the airline into the jet age. For the short term, he procured five DC-7Bs, which were readily available and would launch premium service. For the medium term, he rolled the dice on the British turboprop Vickers Viscount. When they started arriving in 1958, the 15 Viscounts would fly in all-first class configuration and the DC-7Bs would convert to coach on the same routes. And on the day he ordered the Viscounts, Six also committed Continental to four Boeing 707 jetliners.

Six had, in effect, bet the company. The debt burden for the new aircraft left no room for poor financial performance. The pundits claimed that the Chicago–Los Angeles route couldn't support four profitable carriers and predicted the early demise of tiny Continental in the face off with the Big Three. But the pundits were wrong.

The first DC-7B flight from Los Angeles to Chicago launched Continental into a new era in April 1957 with Gold Carpet Service. Passengers were pampered by an exceptionally luxurious interior, superior cuisine, and two lounges, including a men-only Stag Lounge. Continental held its own on the route, and when the Viscounts came, the competition had nothing to match it.

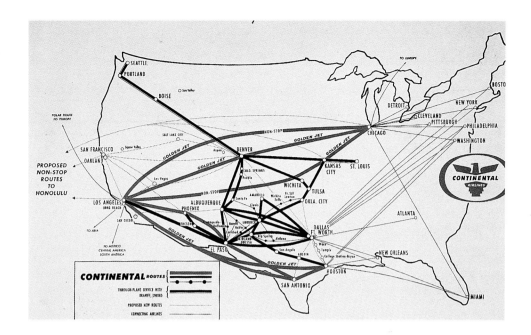

This route map of the early 1960s illustrates how Continental had expanded its regional routes following the breakthrough award of the nonstop Chicago–Los Angeles route in 1955. The heavy lines indicate Golden Jet service with the airline's growing fleet of 707s and 720s. Initially starting with four 707s on the Chicago–Los Angeles routes, Continental doubled their productivity by flying them twice as much per day than the industry norm at the time.

Continental's Viscounts were a stretched, more powerful version of the model introduced to the United States by Capital's earlier massive order of 60 aircraft. Almost 100 miles per hour faster than the DC-7s and smooth as silk by comparison, they drew passengers off the competing piston liners in droves.

Suddenly upstart Continental had over 40 percent of the Chicago-Denver and Los Angeles–Denver markets and in a bit of a stretch claimed to be "First in the West With Jet Powered Flight." The DC-7s flew coach on these routes, getting a leg up on the competition's DC-6s and Constellations. The Viscounts didn't have the range for Chicago–Los Angeles nonstop, but its DC-7s held their own on the route.

Continental's equipment advantage didn't last long, for the jets started arriving the following year. Continental launched jet service on June 8, 1959. It was the third domestic airline to fly its own jet fleet (discounting National's scoop of the field with leased Pan American jets). The pundits were once again skeptical about Continental's chances, claiming that four jets were not enough to provide competitive service. Conventional wisdom held that a

Continental's 707s were Golden Jets, extending the Golden Carpet service theme started on the DC-7s. They had gold tails, gold accents throughout the cabin, and stewardesses in gold uniforms. Later public relations sloganeering renamed them Proud Birds with the Golden Tail.

Continental went to some length to show that economy class passengers also benefited from its high standards of service. Continental had its own food kitchens since the introduction of the Convair 240 in 1948. A greater source of envy to modern-day coach passengers is the generous legroom apparent in this illustration.

GOLDEN JET CLUB COACH MEALS *like this one are colorful and appetizing. Meals in the first-class section are even more sumptuous.*

fleet of 10 was the minimum for success. Once again, Continental proved convention wrong.

Six's solution was to effectively double his 707 fleet by making his jets fly twice the hours per day flown by most other airlines. This feat was considered impossible in those early days of the jet age when nobody knew how remarkably reliable they would prove to be. Continental's four jets maintained a schedule of six round trips a day between Chicago and Los Angeles, three of them nonstop, averaging 15 hours of utilization per day. To insulate itself from having to take a jet out of service for scheduled major maintenance (which would have reduced its fleet by 25 percent), Continental pioneered the concept of progressive maintenance for airliners. It was an idea borrowed from the military, subjecting the jets to continuous intensive maintenance in service, on layovers at suitable maintenance bases, which reduced the need for major downtime.

Continental's 707s were Golden Jets, expanding the propliners' Golden Carpet theme. They had gold tails, the flight attendants sported gold uniforms, and gold accents were liberally applied in the cabin. And they carved out for Continental a profitable, sustainable market share on their competitive routes.

The company ordered a fifth 707, followed by three shorter-range 720Bs for delivery in 1962.

Like most of its competitors, Continental had long been keen to enter the Hawaiian market. It was one of many airlines that applied for Hawaiian authority in 1959, but it would be more than a decade of on-again, off-again hearings before the outcome would be decided. In the meantime, Continental was allowed to serve Los Angeles from Houston and it got considerable Pacific experience by other means.

By 1964, the Vietnam war was heating up and Continental got one of the first Military Airlift Command (MAC) contracts to fly troops and cargo between the United States and Southeast Asia. For the remainder of the decade, the MAC contracts were large enough to justify adding four dedicated Boeing 707-320s to the fleet.

Most U.S. trunk carriers flew military contracts to Southeast Asia but in 1965, Robert Six's adventurous spirit got his airline much closer to harm's way. Continental set up a subsidiary, Continental Air Services (CAS), headquartered in Bangkok, Thailand, with its operations base in Vientiane, Laos. With a ragtag fleet ranging from bush planes through C-47s to DC-6s, it flew cargo and passengers for years throughout Laos, Vietnam, and Cambodia in support of USAID and other government programs. It was a separate entity from Air America but shared its territory and what came with it. Needless to say, most of its pilots weren't 707 senior captains on the Chicago–Los Angeles run who had bid a CAS tour for a change of scenery.

In 1966, 30 years after Six bought into struggling Varney Air Service, Continental portrayed itself as "The Airline That Pride Built," and its jets became "Proud Birds with the Golden Tail." Ignoring innuendoes from the competition linking the gold-uniformed flight attendants to the new publicity campaign, Continental celebrated with a major aircraft purchase. It upped to 19 a previous order for 12 DC-9s intended to replace the Viscounts, signed up for 13 727-200s, and leased 5 727-100s in the interim. Robert Six also took another big chance, betting that Hawaiian service would be approved, and ordered three Boeing 747s.

The following year, Continental built further Pacific experience when it won a contract in association with Hawaiian Airlines and a local development authority to set up and run Air Micronesia to serve the Pacific U.S. Trust Territories spanning an area of ocean almost as large as the United States. Air Mike, as it was affectionately known, initially operated two Boeing 727s and a DC-6B in and out of the islands'

Like Braniff, Continental was one of the first airlines to adopt a widebody look in its 727 fleet when the widebody era took off. The interior could be retrofitted to existing aircraft and became the standard industrywide.

short coral strips, buzzing them before landing to clear the wildlife. Destinations without a strip were served with two float planes.

When Continental's first new Boeing 727s entered service in 1968 they sported a new gold, orange, and black livery and an abstract logo suggesting wide reach and motion. Late that year the Pacific route awards were announced and Continental won rights to Hawaii and beyond, but the whole case got bogged down in politics as Richard Nixon replaced Lyndon Johnson in the White House.

When the smoke cleared the following year, Continental had at last been authorized to serve Hawaii but was denied the routes beyond. The Hawaiian market was made intensely competitive by generous route approvals to several airlines. Nevertheless, Continental enthusiastically started Boeing 707 service to the islands in late 1969. And when in 1970 its first Boeing 747, *The Proud Bird of Seattle*, took off on its inaugural flight from Los Angeles to Honolulu with Bob Six on board, it was one of the airline's crowning moments, an age beyond its first four-passenger Vega's Pueblo–El Paso run three and a half decades before.

Continental ordered a fourth Boeing 747, but as the widebody era matured, it built its widebody capacity around a large fleet of McDonnell Douglas DC-10s that better suited its routes than the 747. The airline continued to be tightly run during the last years of regulation, more successfully weathering the recession, the energy crisis, and the runaway inflation of the 1970s than several of its peers.

Following deregulation, Continental's fortunes took a dramatic turn for the worse when it attracted the attention of airline takeover shark, Frank Lorenzo. By the time the dreaded Lorenzo got through with Continental, he had driven Bob Six's successor to suicide and came to within a hair's breadth of killing the airline as he destroyed Eastern. Even by the viciously tough competitive standards of the 1980s, Lorenzo's business conduct was judged to be so monstrous that he was legally banned by the government from working in the airline industry.

For years, Continental's employees suffered the effects of the Lorenzo period's upheavals. Eventually the wounds began to heal, and today Continental is a thriving, vibrant, international airline. But it is quite a different organization from "The Airline That Pride Built."

Braniff

The restless young World War I veteran must have found it dreadful to sit at his desk in his elder brother's Oklahoma City insurance company after serving as an aircraft gunner in France with the American Expeditionary Force. Finally, the former corporal could take no more. In 1923 he got his pilot's license from Orville Wright, and by the following year, he was barnstorming across Oklahoma in his own World War I surplus Curtiss Jenny. He did everything to make flying pay, including delivering the *Daily Oklahoman* by air to outlying homesteads with a sure toss of the hand. He was Paul Revere Braniff, and over the next decade, together with his brother Tom, he would lay the foundations of one of America's most colorful airlines.

Oil was the name of the game in the Roaring Twenties in the Panhandle, and Paul Braniff realized that the airplane was the perfect mode of transportation for risk-taking oilmen in a hurry across vast, empty spaces. By the spring of 1928, he talked his brother and four wealthy friends into investing in a flying venture to the tune of a cabin class Stinson Detroiter.

On June 20, 1928, the Paul R. Braniff, Inc. Airline was formed offering three daily nonstops between Oklahoma City and Tulsa, Monday through Friday. It was audacious to launch a shoestring airline without an air mail contract in those pioneering days, and it barely lasted a year before Universal Aviation Corporation, a forerunner of American Airways, bought the struggling company.

Paul Braniff took off a year in Mexico to help a friend with a local airline, and by the time he returned, Postmaster General Walter Folger Brown's 1930 spoils conferences had shut off all hopes of an air mail contract for an upstart. But Braniff was determined to get back into the game. The oilmen wanted speed and he would give them airplanes that would outrun the plodding passenger/mail planes. He again convinced brother Tom to open the purse strings, and in November 1930, the newly established Braniff Airways' two slippery Lockheed Vegas commenced service between Tulsa and Wichita Falls via Oklahoma City. Kansas City was next, and by the following year the Vegas sped all the way to Chicago and also branched off to St. Louis.

Other high-spirited independents were working in the oil patch and surrounding areas, and at Braniff's instigation, they banded together into the Independent Scheduled Air Transport Operators Association and hired a lawyer to represent their interests in Washington, D.C. Among them was Bowen Air Lines, operating south of Braniff's territory to Dallas and Houston. "Fly With the Mail" trumpeted the post office slogan to drum up passengers for the contract carriers. "Fly Past the Mail," responded Bowen pushing his swift Vegas.

Braniff operated a fleet of nine DC-6s, the first ones entering service in 1947. Initially they served domestic routes and then also launched Braniff's South American services. The 52 seats on board were convertible to 32 berths for overnight travel. The DC-6 was retired from the Braniff fleet in 1965.

Quite a different image is conveyed by this March 1942 edition of the *B Liner*, the company magazine. Spring is here and company employees are reminded to change over to operating procedures appropriate for the season. The DC-3 in the background is one of 10 Braniff was flying at the time alongside five DC-2s. Half the fleet would soon be appropriated to serve Air Transport Command. During the war, Braniff operated a primarily cargo operation down to Panama and Guatemala called the Banana Run.

In the summer of 1934, Braniff got the break it needed to insure its long-term survival. It was one of the few newcomers to win an air mail contract under the Democrat-sponsored 1934 Air Mail Act that redistributed the mail contracts doled out at the Republican-supported spoils conferences. They were largely returned to the same companies that originally flew them, but Braniff walked off with the lucrative Dallas-Chicago route formerly held by United.

Braniff next picked up the air mail contract between Dallas and Amarillo by acquiring Long and Harmon Airlines, a neighboring independent that won the bid in 1934. With the acquisition came more destinations, and Braniff bought its first Lockheed L-10 Electras to handle the increasing traffic throughout its growing system.

Braniff pounced on another opportunity to expand in 1936 when Bowen Air Lines threw in the towel, giving up its routes to Houston and Brownsville. Less than six years after its gutsy resur-

rection Braniff spanned the country from Chicago to the Mexican border. "Braniff—From the Great Lakes to the Gulf," proclaimed the ads.

The year 1936 also brought the departure of Paul Braniff from the airline to bring Texas its first air conditioners. When the brothers parted ways, Tom Braniff assumed full control and appointed Charles Beard as his right-hand man. Beard would remain with the airline until 1965, rising to the top spot in due course.

By 1937 Braniff was ready to step up to the 21-passenger DC-3s, but none were available. DC-2s on the other hand were plentiful as the Big Four took delivery of their own fleets of DC-3s. They made sense on Braniff's thinner routes, and the airline acquired seven of them secondhand from TWA. The first went into service in June 1937, and with it came Braniff's first stewardesses whom the airline, like TWA, preferred to call hostesses.

Two years later the first DC-3s joined the fleet, and by 1942, Braniff was operating a 15-strong Douglas fleet of 5 DC-2s and 10 DC-3s. It didn't come close to the Big Four, but it was bigger than Continental, Delta, and Northwest. But its fleet was about to be cut in half by World War II as Air Transport Command claimed the B-liners on contract to haul personnel and supplies.

Braniff's primary assignment during the war was the Banana Run from San Antonio down to Central America, terminating in Guatemala and Panama and serving points in between. The B-Line also did its share of pilot and mechanic training during the war, and in 1942, it carried out a plan it had been contemplating for some time when it moved its headquarters from Oklahoma City to the brighter lights of Dallas.

The war broadened Braniff's horizons and it flew the Banana Run for more than two years without an accident. But the experience would pale in comparison to the postwar challenge the small southern regional was about to have thrust upon it as a result of a long simmering feud between Pan American and W. R. Grace and Company, the co-owners of Panagra, which dominated the western half of South America.

W. R. Grace and Company had long wanted to extend Panagra's routes up into the United States, but Pan American had bluntly cut off any access beyond Panama to protect its own interests. Because the partnership was an even split, W. R. Grace was powerless and the relationship deteriorated into an increasingly public falling-out between the two parties by the end of World War II.

Into this picture came the President, Harry S. Truman, convinced by the U.S. State Department that the fight was anticompetitive and mocked America's standing south of the border. Truman, not the greatest fan of big business, decided that spoiled Pan American needed a little competition. In 1946 he instructed the CAB to "put" Braniff into South America. The small regional carrier that had just started a modest service to neighboring Mexico found itself a major international airline. Overnight it had over 20,000 miles of foreign routes ranging from Houston all the way down to Rio de Janeiro, Brazil, and Buenos Aires, Argentina, via Lima, Peru, across the towering Andes Mountains—at least on paper.

Pan American, who had already taken Braniff's Mexican insurrection as a personal insult, unleashed its formidable resources to obstruct the challenge. Braniff aircraft flying to Mexico suddenly found the radio ranges mysteriously malfunctioning whenever they were in the vicinity. Airports were shut down and the gas pumps closed when they arrived. And in late 1946, the Mexican government abruptly cancelled Braniff's operating certificate.

The company didn't fare much better in its initial attempts to acquire local authorizations to operate its new South American routes. Applications were inexplicably delayed, rules and fees kept changing abruptly, and insurance requirements became a moving target. But Braniff persevered and in June 1948, renamed Braniff International Airways, it reached Lima, Peru, with its first modern, pressurized airliner, the DC-6. Naming the service Conquistador may well have been an inside joke. The following year Conquistador service pushed on to Rio de Janeiro, and by 1950, Braniff was flying all the way to Buenos Aires.

From Lima, Braniff branched off to La Paz, Bolivia, at 14,000 feet, the world's highest airport. The route was first flown by DC-3s, which were soon replaced by DC-4s equipped with jet-assisted takeoff (JATO) packs to boost their takeoff performance in La Paz's rarefied atmosphere. The JATO packs, mounted under the wings, produced a sizzling climb rate and a fiery departure.

Meanwhile, closer to home the company reestablished full domestic operations with DC-3s and an increasing number of C-54s converted to civilian DC-4 layout. The first of six DC-6s joined the fleet in 1947, and by 1950, they were providing sleeper service from Houston and Dallas to Chicago.

Braniff accomplished several firsts among U.S. airlines in the postwar years. It was the first airline

The image of the Conquistador became the enduring symbol of Braniff's South American operations. Considering the underhanded campaign Pan American waged to delay Braniff's entry into the market, the name may well be an inside joke.

RIO

it's

BRANIFF

An early 1950s poster promotes Braniff's service to Rio de Janeiro via Lima, Peru. Although the airline was awarded the South American routes in 1946, it didn't reach Rio until 1949, followed by Buenos Aires a year later. *Don Thomas Foundation*

to be certified to use the instrument landing system, which the government began installing in the summer of 1947. And in 1952, it was the first airliner to put in service the Convair 340, a stretched, more powerful upgrade of the CV 240. The airline ordered 20 of these versatile short- to mid-range aircraft and used them to gradually replace its DC-3s and DC-4s. Later the Convair fleet was joined by five CV 440 Metropolitans.

In 1952 Braniff further solidified its position in the middle section of the country with the acquisition of Kansas City-based Mid Continent

Airlines. The transaction brought new routes as far as Minneapolis, Minnesota, to the north and New Orleans, Louisiana, to the south. Mid Continent's 23 DC-3s and 4 Convair 240s were integrated into the Braniff fleet.

The year 1954 brought a changing of the guard at Braniff's helm when Tom Braniff tragically perished in the crash of a Grumman Mallard amphibian returning from a duck-hunting trip. Charles Beard, who was largely responsible for developing Braniff's South American operations, assumed the reins. The first big prize Braniff received under his tenure was authorization by the CAB to serve New York City in 1956. His first big challenge was to manage Braniff's transition to the jet age.

On the eve of the jet age, Braniff put in service the last great propliner, the DC-7C, attracted by the performance of its turbo-compound engines at the airline's high-altitude South American stops and over the Andes. The Seven Seas featured Silver Service on El Dorado flights, an ironic choice of name in hindsight after the aircraft proved to be only marginally profitable because of high engine maintenance costs. The aircraft also flew the domestic routes and a DC-7C displayed its long reach by inaugurating Braniff's nonstop Miami–Rio de Janeiro service in 1959, but by then its days were numbered.

Braniff took a conventional approach to transitioning to jets. For its medium-haul routes, which were ideal for turboprops, it chose the Lockheed L-188 Electra. For its long-haul routes it managed to convince Boeing to custom build it an especially powerful version of the original production 707, the 227, by equipping the five Braniff airplanes with the more powerful JT-4 engines instead of the standard JT-3s to better handle the South American high-altitude airports. For a time Braniff could claim in its advertising that it had the fastest jetliner in the business.

Braniff's smooth, powerful Lockheed Electras entered service in June 1959 to an enthusiastic reception until tragedy struck three months later. A Braniff Electra disintegrated in excellent weather shortly after climbing out of Houston. The accident baffled investigators. The aircraft involved had been delivered by Lockheed only 10 days before, and the global Electra fleet had accumulated over 80,000 hours of trouble-free experience in every conceivable condition.

The mystery wouldn't be solved for more than a year and not before a Northwest Electra suffered the same fate. The problem proved to be an insufficiently strong longeron in the engine nacelle that failed to dampen vibration under certain rare conditions and

This conservatively attired matron of the skies seems a century apart from the miniskirt-clad gogo stewardesses of the flower power age to come.

caused the nacelle to flutter leading to catastrophic wing failure.

The FAA didn't ground the Electra but restricted it to the speed of the piston liners until the problem was solved. The airlines had to work hard to rehabilitate the Electra's reputation, but it went on to a solid career and its Navy patrol version, the Lockheed P-3 Orion continued to serve into the twenty-first century.

Braniff also had bad luck with its first 707, which crashed before it had a chance to join the fleet, but in this case the cause was pilot error. Its mixed Braniff-Boeing crew was maneuvering on a test flight the day before delivery and lost control of

Now! only on **BRANIFF**

WORLD'S FASTEST JETLINER!

Fastest between New York or Chicago and Texas

exclusively on Braniff
the Different and Superior
BOEING 707·227
...the JET with the BIG engines

El Dorado Super Jet ®

FASTEST--cruises over 600 m.p.h.
POWER PLUS--20% to 40% more
ON·TIME--the most power in reserve
EPICURE MEALS--Braniff's famed service
ELEGANT LUXURY--decor exclusively Braniff's

(Both first class and tourist.)

coming soon to
South America
world's fastest
jetliner!

BRANIFF *International* AIRWAYS

Call any Braniff office or your travel agent. General Offices: Dallas, Texas.

Equipped with the JT-4 engines, Braniff's 707-227s were the fastest jetliners for a time, a fact the airline emphasized in its advertising. Although destined for the South American network, the 707 was conservatively introduced on the prestigious domestic Dallas-Chicago route.

a dutch roll. But the second ship wasn't far behind on the delivery schedule and Braniff became a jet carrier on December 19, 1959, by inaugurating Boeing 707 service between Dallas and New York. By the spring of the following year, the 707s were also serving South America.

Like many of its contemporaries, Braniff felt the acute need for a medium-range jet. In 1960 it selected the only readily available U.S. alternative, the Boeing 720. The following year, to serve shorter-range needs, it became the first U.S. airline to order the twin-engined, British Aircraft Corporation BAC 111. The B-720s began arriving in 1961, but the 12 BAC 111s didn't enter service until 1965, delayed somewhat by problems at the manufacturer.

As the mid-1960s approached, Braniff was perceived as a stable, conservative company with an attractive route system that did a fair job of the business it had, but wasn't particularly aggressive about further growth. Its situation attracted the attention of the Dallas-based insurer, Greatamerica Corporation, whose entrepreneurial managers sensed an opportunity to pick up an underutilized business and greatly increase its value by pushing it to realize its full potential. In 1964 Greatamerica acquired majority control of Braniff, and the following year, it installed Harding Lawrence, Bob Six's right-hand man at fast-paced, innovative Continental, to run it. The effect on Braniff was explosive.

Lawrence rushed to file additional route applications and conclude an order for 18 aircraft that had been prepared before his arrival and included Boeing 707-320C Intercontinentals and Braniff's first Boeing 727s. But the initiative that propelled Braniff into the national consciousness was a massive, brilliant image overhaul dubbed "The End of the Plain Plane."

The campaign was created by Mary Wells, one of Madison Avenue's hottest young stars, and it splashed the psychedelic sixties all over one of America's most conservative airlines. The center-piece of Wells' campaign was repainting each aircraft in a choice of seven dazzling solid colors. She also hired Italian fashion designer Emilio Pucci to devise a new hostess wardrobe and interior designer Alexander Girard to redo the aircraft interiors and ground facilities. Pucci's couture transformed the stewardess uniform into a fashion statement. Girard provided the airborne catwalk.

The campaign electrified the popular imagination. Braniff flooded the national media. Nicknames, the best measure of lasting attention, spread like wildfire. Braniff was flying the Easter egg planes, or

Soon after Harding Lawrence assumed the helm at Braniff in 1965, he made the decision to standardize the domestic fleet. His choice was the most versatile airliner of the era, the Boeing 727, which could make a profit on routes from 150 miles to 2,000 miles. The selection of the 727 coincided with Braniff's "The End of the Plain Plane" campaign, which presented each Braniff aircraft in one of seven dazzling colors and featured designer stewardess clothing and interiors.

SOUTH AMERICA BRANIFF STYLE

the jelly bean fleet. The flight attendants were Pucci Galores (*Goldfinger* was hot that year), and when they shed layers of their outfits in flight to more easily perform their various tasks, they were doing the Braniff air strip. The campaign encouraged the sexy image. "Does your wife know you are flying with us?" asked one punch line.

The public flocked on board. Fleet utilization soared, and within a year of Lawrence's arrival, profits doubled. Braniff's stock, stable at $24 when Lawrence took the helm, breathlessly shot past $120. Lawrence and Wells got married and became the prototype power couple. Their gain was Braniff's loss, for Wells' agency resigned the Braniff account on conflict of interest grounds and was hired by TWA.

In 1967 Braniff completed a major coup in Latin America that had been pending for several years. It bought its rival, Panagra. The Pan American–W. R. Grace feud had deteriorated to a point where Grace was willing to sell, even to Pan Am. The CAB, however, disapproved, favoring Braniff to keep Pan

American's South American influence in check. With the purchase came seven Super DC-8-62s Panagra had ordered and Braniff decided to keep.

Braniff continued to place further B-727 orders for domestic use and in 1967 made the decision to standardize its fleet around the type. The B-707 Intercontinentals, which were primarily ferrying U.S. troops on military charter contracts between the United States and the Far East, were the last early jets to go, sold off as the Vietnam War wound down.

In 1969 the long-awaited right to serve Hawaii from Dallas was finally granted, and Braniff was ready, after all those military charters across the Pacific. Service was established with the airline's B-707s, but in anticipation of the award an order had already been placed in 1968 for two Boeing 747s exclusively for the Hawaiian route. In January 1971, a giant orange Jumbo Jet became queen of the Braniff fleet. "747 Braniff Place—The most exclusive address in the sky," announced the ads, but it was the Great Pumpkin to the masses and Fat Al to some of its pilots.

The Great Pumpkin never got its stable mate because as widebody capacity flooded the market, Braniff cancelled the order. For years it plied its route between Dallas and Hawaii, seven days a week, 15 hours aloft per round trip, pioneering long-haul widebody utilization rates that would become standard only in later, meaner years.

When the smaller widebodies appeared, Braniff chose to stick with the 727s and the lonely Great Pumpkin. It turned out to be a judicious choice in the short run, for overcapacity quickly developed as all the airlines jumped on the bandwagon and then the 1973 oil crisis hit with a vengeance.

As the 1970s progressed, Braniff was well positioned to continue prospering and the company's optimistic mood persisted. When deregulation came, the hard-charging Lawrence saw it as Braniff's big chance to turn into a global airline. Rapid growth was the key to survival in his view, and he led Braniff on a frenzy of expansion on borrowed funds to grab market share.

Braniff fanned out across the United States with new routes, strengthened its South American position, started service to scores of destinations in Asia and Europe, and built a sleek new headquarters in Dallas to manage it all. The Great Pumpkin was joined at last by a fleet of fellow 747s, and the dream was alive.

But it was unsustainable. Recession eroded passenger volumes, fare wars destroyed profit margins, interest rates shot up to over 20 percent, and the debt load became unmanageable. In 1982 Braniff crashed, destroying the lives of thousands of loyal employees. It was the first of the classic American airlines to fall and with it went the thrilling, romantic, and at times uncertain adventure that started when Paul Braniff hauled a Stinson Detroiter aloft on its first revenue flight.

Braniff acquired a sole Boeing 747 in 1971 to serve the Dallas-Hawaii route for which the airline won authority in 1969. Named "747 Braniff Place" by the airline, it was the "Great Pumpkin" to most of the media and passengers and "Fat Al" to most of its pilots. Braniff briefly operated additional 747s during its post-deregulation frenzy of expansion.

National

Captain Eddie Rickenbacker, president of Eastern Airlines, had a short fuse and an intense distaste for National and its bulldog founder and president, Ted Baker. Addressing a group that included Baker in Mobile, Alabama, during the 1930s, and frustrated by National's encroachment into territory Rickenbacker viewed as rightfully belonging to Eastern, he is said to have stared at his adversary and declared "Some people are trying to pirate our routes in the South!" A delighted Baker instantly christened National's route network The Buccaneer Route. He painted the term in bold letters on the fuselage of his airplanes and splashed it all over National's schedules and posters, complete with a swashbuckling pirate figure wielding a sword who seemed to be personally looking for Captain Eddie.

Rickenbacker, whose bitter feud with Ted Baker became an industry legend, wasn't far from the truth. Before moving to the South, Baker's Chicago-based National Airlines Taxi System did a thriving business flying thirsty clients to Canada on rum runs during prohibition. The repeal of prohibition also repealed National's profits and Baker had to look for alternative sources of revenue. When the Air Mail Act of 1934 put up the air mail routes for new bids, Baker decided the future lay in being subsidized by Uncle Sam.

The one time repo man audaciously bid for two routes, Cleveland-Nashville and St. Petersburg–Daytona Beach. To his surprise, he won the 146-mile run over the Florida swamps between St. Petersburg and Daytona Beach. The only other bidder was a group of Tampa worthies who incorporated themselves as Gulf Airlines but had no airplanes and no clue about running an air service. Eastern's failure to bid on the route was a stunning oversight that would come back to haunt it in the years ahead.

On October 15, 1934, National Airlines System's two Ryan monoplanes officially started daily service from St. Pete to Daytona Beach via Tampa, Lakeland, and Orlando to feed Eastern's north-south air mail route running along the East Coast. From these modest, and relatively late beginnings National would grow into one of the most colorful trunk carriers of the United States and claim a disproportionate share of air transportation "firsts" in coming years.

But in the meantime, crises would have to be overcome and the first one struck shortly after the inaugural mail run. More passengers turned up than seats were available for them in the two Ryans. Additional capacity was needed, made more urgent by rumblings from dormant Gulf Airlines about commencing operations. Baker scrambled to replace the Ryans with three Stinson Trimotors, to ease any

A nice portrait of a National DC-7B. Note the black radar dome and the old-fashioned, streamlined automatic direction finder loop antenna housing. The DC-7B was an effective competitor to the Lockheed Super Constellation in the duel of the piston liners.

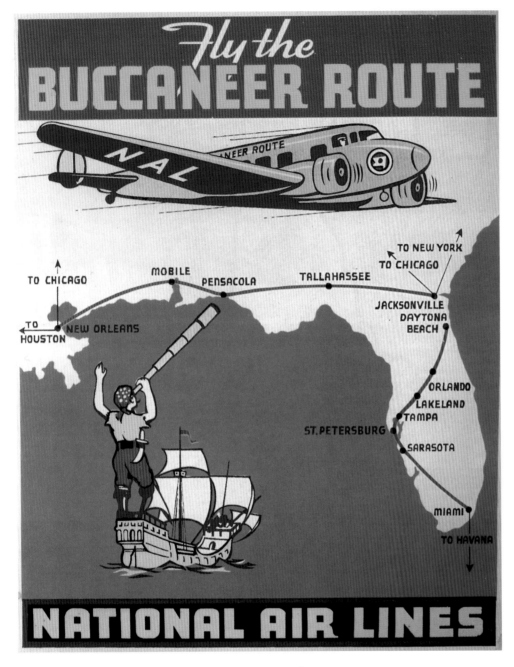

Fly the **BUCCANEER ROUTE**

NATIONAL AIR LINES

National Airlines had a tempestuous relationship with its much bigger rival, Eastern, from its earliest days. The Buccaneer Route theme featured on this counter card was adopted when Eastern's president Eddie Rickenbacker is said to have accused National of trying to pirate some of its routes. *Don Thomas Foundation.*

doubts about National's commitment and capabilities. He also started merger negotiations with Gulf Airlines, to eliminate its threat. But he characteristically dragged his foot, finally signing the merger papers after almost two years of continuous wrangling.

Another crisis came in early 1935, when an Eastern DC-2 crashed on takeoff on Daytona's marginal runway and Eastern was allowed to temporarily suspend service to Daytona until the runway was extended. All of a sudden National was unplugged from the air mail system. To get around having to carry the mail to the next stop over land, Baker asked for and was granted temporary rights on the Daytona-Jacksonville route, successfully arguing that his smaller aircraft could safely use Daytona's airport.

The temporary extension gave National valuable operational experience and credibility, which didn't go unnoticed when in July 1937, it won rights from St. Petersburg to Miami via Sarasota and Fort Myers. This route justified a step up in equipment and the company acquired its first sleek, 10-passenger Lockheed 10 Electra, featuring all the modern advances of the day's aviation technology. It was soon followed by three other Electras as National solidified its hold in the Florida market.

In 1938 Baker fended off a serious challenge from Eastern, which had applied for the Atlanta-Miami route via St. Petersburg to link up with Pan American's Latin American service, threatening National's St. Petersburg–Miami leg. At local public hearings a Baker ally politely badgered Rickenbacker to explain why Eastern couldn't terminate the Atlanta flight at Tampa, finally prompting the captain to lose his temper and yell, "Because Tampa is a dead-end town!" Eastern was turned down.

At the same time, both National and Eastern applied for the Jacksonville, Florida–New Orleans, Louisiana, route via Tallahassee, Pensacola, and Mobile, Alabama. Eastern was confident in its application, because National had returned to the Daytona Beach–Jacksonville route when the Daytona airport was lengthened, leaving the Buccaneer line with a land gap in its proposed route network. But the CAB, no friend of Eastern, gave the nod to National.

Baker promptly moved National's headquarters to Jacksonville, extracting the construction of a free hangar from the town fathers, and lobbied hard for rights over the Daytona-Jacksonville gap.

In March 1940 the gap was closed and National celebrated with the purchase of its first factory-new airplanes, two L-18 Lockheed Lodestars joined by a third one the following year. The 14-passenger Lodestars were 90 knots faster than the DC-3s and were the first aircraft in National's fleet to carry flight attendants and offer onboard meals.

In only six years National had become an established, respected regional carrier. The Buccaneer Route resembled a reverse S from New Orleans across to Jacksonville, down to St. Petersburg and across again to Miami, as if slashed into the map by a pirate's sword. It looked as if National was set to settle down to flying its hard-won routes, but Baker was ever on the make and World War II was about to give him his biggest break.

Like the rest of the nation's airlines, National was keen to contribute to the war effort. Its swift Lodestars were pressed into domestic cargo service for Air Transport Command, and it also flew other aircraft on contract with the military. Equally important was its training contribution. The company ran training schools for military flight crews and mechanics. The tight-fisted Baker managed to get himself in trouble with the military by using some trainees from National's contract schools as unpaid crew members on the airline's remaining civilian passenger runs. Always spoiling for an argument, he indignantly claimed he was only being generous, giving the raw cadets free hands-on experience.

As the war entered its final phase and the airlines began jockeying fiercely to position themselves for the postwar world, Baker pulled off a coup that overnight transformed National from a small, regional carrier into an airline befitting its name. Competition was becoming a popular word at the CAB and in February 1944, National won approval to operate scheduled service between Jacksonville and New York City. The buccaneer had found the buried treasure.

New York–Miami Lodestar service was finally launched in October 1944. Norfolk, Wilmington, Charleston, and Savannah were also included in the new route award and were gradually added to the schedules as more Lodestars were released to National from military service. By the end of 1945, 11 Lodestars were in the National fleet, later joined by three more.

The twice-daily Miami–New York Lodestar flights were doing a good job, but Baker knew that it would take more than that for National to make it on the Eastern-dominated East Coast route. Eastern wasn't unduly alarmed about National's expansion into the market. The Great Silver Fleet would be flying Constellations on the route and until they arrived sometime in 1946, the DC-3s would nicely hold the buccaneer fleet at bay. But Eastern was in for a nasty surprise.

While many other airlines were converting wartime C-54s to passenger configuration, Baker had discovered that Douglas had a backlog of almost completed C-54s that could be quickly finished as civilian DC-4s at a bargain price. He signed up for seven of them and, on Valentine's Day 1946, National became the first airline to operate nonstop between New York and Miami, in a shiny, new 44-seat DC-4. The irascible Baker had scooped Eastern's nonstop service by almost a year. The flight was, of course, called *The Buccaneer*.

Baker's next act was to crack pepper under Juan Trippe's nose. He took National international, right into Pan American's back yard. In December 1946 National inaugurated service to Havana, Cuba, from Miami and Tampa. The route turned out to be a gold mine as straight-laced Americans flocked in droves to pre-Castro Havana to let their hair down. The Havana run kept National comfortably profitable throughout the 1950s, offsetting periodic financial pressures on its domestic routes. In the last two years before the Communist takeover, National even operated nonstop flights between New York and Havana.

The unpressurized DC-4s were soon followed into service by pressurized DC-6s, the first of which was introduced in mid-1947. National was in the ascent with no end in sight, when Ted Baker's abrasive character and tight-fisted treatment of his employees triggered a chain of events that almost destroyed his airline.

Baker's famous stinginess contributed greatly to National's success and it was his employees who bore the brunt of his parsimony. To protect themselves, they unionized with a vengeance and by

The Lockheed L-18 Lodestar became National's airliner of choice as soon as it could afford them. The 14-passenger Lodestars were 90 knots faster than the DC-3. They were the first National aircraft to carry stewardesses and onboard meals.

Ted Baker moved quickly after World War II to acquire DC-4s, enabling National to be the first to offer nonstop New York to Miami service, scooping Eastern by nearly a year.

January 1948, they had had enough. National was struck by the International Association of Machinists, representing the station workers and clerical staff. Within a month they were joined by the pilots, represented by the Airline Pilots' Association, which had its own feud with Baker about a dismissed pilot.

Instead of compromising to quickly settle the strike, Baker reacted with characteristic belligerence. Unemployed wartime pilots were a dime a dozen, and National hired them in droves to replace the strikers. The mood turned ugly, fistfights broke out on the picket lines, and an instructor for the new hires was murdered. (The case was never solved, so it is not known whether the strike was responsible, but it didn't help cool tensions on the picket line.)

The striking pilots mounted a highly organized national campaign calling on passengers to boycott National and profits plummeted. The strike went on for five months, but by the time both parties decided to end it, it had triggered a more sinister threat to the

airline, the Civil Aviation Board's Docket 3500, the National Airlines Dismemberment Case.

The case alleged that National was too weakened financially to continue as a going concern. The public interest would be better served if it were forced out of existence and its assets divided among its competitors. The motivation was political. Harry Truman was badly trailing Thomas E. Dewey in the 1948 presidential elections and needed every union vote he could get. It is generally accepted among historians that a backroom deal was made. National would be dismembered in exchange for the union vote.

Although initiated by the unions, Pan American and Panagra also quickly got on the Docket 3500 supporters' bandwagon, seeing it as a golden opportunity to at last acquire access to the coveted domestic routes extending all the way up to New York. But although Pan Am owned 50 percent of Panagra, the relationship was an acrimonious one, in part because Pan Am refused Panagra access to U.S. gateway cities.

NATIONAL ★ Airlines

Presents THE *Star* ★
DC-6 Luxury Plus!

Airline of the Stars

THROUGH FLIGHTS to

California

and all the West

<u>NO</u> CHANGE OF PLANE

AMERICAN AIRLINES

Delta AIR LINES

NATIONAL AIRLINES

Shortest ... Fastest DC-6 Luxury All The Way

In 1950 the Buccaneer line became the Airline of the Stars as National reveled in its East Coast respectability flying from New York to Miami and down to Havana, Cuba. The stars were allegedly from New York's theaters escaping to relax on National's home turf. By then National was flying pressurized DC-6's to counter Eastern's Constellations.

This interchange brochure advertises through service to California from the East Coast on three cooperating airlines with no change of plane. the same DC-6 was flown by crews of each airline through its respective segment of the route from Miami to Los Angeles and San Francisco with points in between.

The wily Baker immediately saw that the best defense was to play off against each other, Pan American and W. R. Grace, Panagra's other shareholder. Both companies began acquiring National shares craftily rationed by Baker, and long after the strike was over and Truman was in the White House, they both realized that the chief buccaneer had engineered a stalemate. Like good poker players, they knew when to fold, and National was in the clear. Docket 3500 lingered on in the CAB bureaucracy until 1951 when it was quietly dismissed.

The late 1940s and the 1950s saw Florida change from a sleepy, seasonal tourist spot into a major year-round destination, and the airlines played a big role in the transformation. The East Coast airlines always had a tough time in the off-season and were looking for ways to redress the traffic imbalance. Heavy summer discounting might fill their planes, but a problem remained. The off-season was so slow that Florida's hotels simply closed down.

In 1949 all that changed. Based on the airlines' promise to deliver sufficient numbers of guests to

National started serving Havana in late 1946 from Miami and Tampa, to Pan American's great displeasure. Straight-laced Americans flocked eagerly to Havana to let their hair down. It proved to be one of National's most profitable destinations, keeping the company afloat through domestic business cycles. By the time of the Cuban revolution, National was even operating nonstop New York–Havana flights.

FLY NATIONAL AIRLINES TO GAY

HAVANA

NATIONAL Airlines
Airline of the Stars

turn a profit, many of the hotels decided to remain open for the first time on a trial basis. National's aggressive marketing efforts played an important role, and the experiment was a success. The north-south routes would always remain seasonal but slowly the airlines were able to build enough summer volume to ease their off-season headaches.

By the end of the 1940s, postwar air coach was coming into use and National joined the trend in 1950 with night coach service followed by day coach a year later. Package holidays complete with hotel accommodations and car rentals became increasingly popular as the economy prospered and mass tourism soon replaced first class travel as the airlines' chief source of revenue.

Like most pirates who last long enough to turn respectable, Baker decided that it was time for an image change more in tune with National's elevated status. In 1950 the Buccaneer line became the Airline of the Stars and its airplanes were adorned with an elegant new red, white, and blue livery featuring a big star on the fuselage. Stars and starlets arriving on National's flights from New York were snapped deplaning in sunny Florida, subtly enticing the middle classes to live the affordable high life. Profits soared, and in 1952 National Airlines went off federal subsidy.

The 1950s saw the addition of more DC-6Bs and DC-7s. On the shorter routes Convair 340s and 440s joined the fleet, and toward the end of the decade National even acquired four of the latest Lockheed Constellations, the 1649H Starliner, convertible between passenger and cargo use. Peace was made with Panagra and Pan Am, and the airlines started a through-plane interchange between New York and Central and South America.

But as the decade neared its end, jets were the new name of the game, and they gave Ted Baker the opportunity to pull off his most spectacular coup. National became the first U.S. airline to offer domestic jet service. It was a typical Baker deal. Finding himself down the priority list at Boeing because he left negotiations too late, he became the first to place a firm order for the Douglas DC-8. The 707, however, would beat the DC-8 into service by about a year, and Baker wasn't about to wait.

He contacted Juan Trippe and proposed leasing two 707s during the winter months when Pan American's transatlantic traffic was low. He enticed Trippe by offering Pan American a large chunk of National stock, holding out once again the possibility of a merger. Baker banked on the CAB turning down any merger proposal while Trippe, perpetually desperate for a domestic foothold, decided to gamble. Baker got his 707s.

And so, on December 10, 1958, National's inaugural Boeing 707 Jet Star flight from New York to Miami became the first domestic jet service in America. Never mind that the jet was in Pan American colors and in a few months it would have to be returned, or that National's own first jet wouldn't be delivered

until early 1960. Baker had beaten American, the next airline to introduce jets on the domestic market, by 45 days. More importantly, he beat Eastern's turboprop Electras into service with a pure jet. He was also right about the CAB. It flatly ruled out any merger proposal between National and Pan American.

Concurrent with DC-8 deliveries, National's Convairs were replaced by Lockheed L-188 Electras, matching rival Eastern's fleet structure, and National prospered. In the summer of 1961 it accomplished a lifetime goal when it inaugurated transcontinental service from Florida on its recently awarded routes to San Francisco and Los Angeles. But Ted Baker had one last surprise. In 1962 he abruptly sold National. Eighteen months later he died of a heart attack.

National's new president and controlling shareholder was Bud Maytag. Heir to the washing machine fortune, he had just sold Frontier Airlines to take on the challenge of running a trunk line. He couldn't have been more different from his predecessor. Down to earth and even-tempered, he brought stability and a much needed professional corporate management style to National. Under his sure, fair hand the airline entered the second phase in its history that would prove to be its golden years.

The Airline of the Stars motif was replaced by a more subtle corporate look, and National entered a period of stable, steady growth. In 1964 the airline became the first all-jet U.S. trunk carrier when the first Boeing 727s joined the DC-8s and turboprop Electras on the flight line and the last of the piston fleet was retired. Boeing 727-200s and the first of two stretched DC-8-61s were introduced in 1967.

By 1968 the flower child generation was in full bloom. Tie dyes, primary colors, and long hair were in; earnest, short-haired men in black suits and skinny black ties were out. Following Braniff's lead, National decided it was a time for a splash of color on the airways and the airline underwent a radical cosmetic facelift.

One of National's first DC-8s. Although National opted for DC-8s, which were a year behind the Boeing 707, it scooped the domestic industry with scheduled jet service on December 10, 1958, by launching Boeing 707 service for the winter season between New York and Miami with two 707s short-leased from Pan American.

Centerpiece of the new look was the Sun King motif symbolizing National's link to Florida, the hedonistic Sunshine State. Instant Florida was the new slogan and flight attendants swapped the traditional stewardess look for bright yellow, lime, and orange dresses sporting racy, short hemlines. "We took Florida and turned it into an airline" read the ad copy.

In 1969 National began flying between Atlanta and San Francisco in competition with Delta. In 1970 it once again became an international airline, establishing historic nonstop service between Miami and London, England. National became the third U.S. airline to cross the Atlantic besides Pan American and TWA, which had monopolized U.S. transatlantic service after American Overseas Airline's sale to Pan Am in 1950.

National had the routes to justify widebody service and promptly put two 747s on the flight line in the fall of 1970. The jumbo jets plied the airways from Miami to New York and Los Angeles, and for three years provided summer service to London. A year after the introduction of the 747s, National also took delivery of the first of nine DC-10-10s, which were later joined by four DC-10-30s. The DC-8s were gradually phased out, and as the DC-10's smaller capacity proved more suitable for National's system, after six years the two 747s were also sold.

In 1971, Bud Maytag's National pulled off an ad campaign worthy of Ted Baker the original buccaneer. The picture of a sexy young flight attendant appeared in the national media with the slogan "I'm Linda. Fly me." Several flight attendants lent their faces and first names to the slogan and National's airplanes were named after them.

The times they were still a'changing and the ensuing uproar was big enough to make *Time* magazine. Feminists picketed with signs advising National to go fly itself. Passions ran high on both sides of the divided passenger pool, ensuring a level of publicity exceeded only by Braniff's "The End of the Plain Plane" campaign.

National continued to do well until deregulation when its relatively small size and good performance made it a takeover target, attracting the attention of several bidders including its old nemesis, Eastern and Frank Lorenzo's Texas International Airlines. Ultimately the winner was Pan American. In 1980, long after Juan Trippe was gone, his airline had its domestic routes. The incorporation of National was badly handled causing much resentment and by then Pan American was terminally ill. When it finally expired after a long, painful struggle it also spirited away the last traces of the Buccaneer line.

National had two Boeing 747s and flew them from Florida to New York and the West Coast. It also launched summer service from Miami to London with them, becoming the third transatlantic U.S. airline behind Pan American and TWA. National's 747s served the airline for six years before being replaced by DC-10s more suitable to passenger volumes on its routes.

Western

On April 27, 1973, Western Airlines took delivery of its first McDonnell Douglas DC-10. Among the passengers on the delivery flight to Los Angeles International Airport was a frail old man who attracted the greatest applause when he disembarked. He was Fred W. Kelly, the 1912 Olympic gold medallist in the 110-meter hurdles and in his time one of the greatest athletes of the University of Southern California. But he was being applauded for another reason. Almost half a century before, he had been the first pilot hired by Western, America's oldest airline to survive into the 1970s under its own name. And the first airplane he flew for Western was the 110-miles per hour open-cockpit fabric-covered Douglas M-2 biplane, a direct ancestor of the massive DC-10.

The airline that flew its first widebody to its Los Angeles home base that day started life in the same city as Western Air Express (WAE) on July 13, 1925. Backed by prominent Los Angeles residents who wanted to avoid the potential ignominy of a future transcontinental air route terminating in San Francisco, it was organized and managed by a former race car driver and local car dealer, Harris M. "Pop" Hanshue.

WAE's first accomplishment was winning the Los Angeles to Salt Lake City air mail route via Las Vegas. It started serving the route in April 1926 and carried its first passengers the following month, on two jump seats in the Douglas M-2's half-ton capacity mail hold.

In 1927 the fears of Western's Los Angeles backers were realized. The main transcontinental mail route was established connecting San Francisco with Chicago and points beyond, and was awarded to Boeing Air Transport, which would eventually become United Airlines. But they had formed their own airline for just such a contingency and the following year, it was able to respond under the auspices of the Guggenheim Fund for the Promotion of Aeronautics.

The fund appointed Western to operate what it called the Model Airway, an experiment to promote California air transportation by linking Los Angeles with San Francisco. Equipped with three Fokker F-10 Trimotors, the first used by a U.S. airline, Western commenced the first air service between the two cities on May 26, 1928. Limousine service between the airport and the city centers, in-flight box lunches served by stewards, and personal log books for passengers enticed pioneering travelers to take to the air. The experiment was a success, transforming Western Air Express from an air mail service into a passenger line.

Western spread its wings aggressively under Hanshue's guiding hand, primarily through the acquisition of smaller fry. Among them was Standard

The DC-10 was Western's first widebody. It replaced the 707s on the Hawaiian flights, and also relieved the pressure on the airline's high-density routes to the midwest and along the West Coast.

Western Air Express' first air mail pilot Fred Kelly poses with an adventurous Hollywood starlet prior to takeoff on the Los Angeles–Salt Lake City route. Kelly was on board Western's first DC-10 on its delivery flight from Long Beach, California.

This rare 1937 baggage sticker features Western Air Express' early Indian head logo. The National Parks Route is reference to Western's purchase of National Parks Airways flying between Salt Lake City and Great Falls, Montana.

WESTERN
AIR
Express
National Parks Route

Airlines linking Los Angeles and El Paso, Texas, founded by Jack Frye who would go on to head TWA. Other acquisitions included the Cheyenne-Pueblo air mail run via Denver, amphibian service to Catalina Island from Los Angeles, and service to Portland and Seattle.

Western also started service to Albuquerque, New Mexico, and pushed the route on to Amarillo, from where it branched to Dallas, Tulsa, and Kansas City. The El Paso terminus was extended to Fort Worth. It also established a subsidiary, Mid-Continent Air Express, linking Denver and El Paso and connecting to the parent company's system.

Pop Hanshue had built quite an empire in the sky by 1930, served by a fleet of 21 Fokker F-10s and assorted other aircraft, but it had a major flaw. Only two routes, Los Angeles–Salt Lake City, and Cheyenne-Pueblo were air mail runs. And without a mail subsidy, the web of routes looked impressive on the map but were hemorrhaging red ink financially. By the middle of 1930, less than a year after most of the frenzied expansion took place, Western Air Express came crashing down with a little help from Postmaster General Walter Folger Brown.

Without a doubt, the big loser in the 1930 reorganization of the transcontinental air mail routes under the auspices of the Watres-McNary Act was Western Air Express. Hanshue was flatly told by Brown that he had no option but to merge most of WEA's operations into Transcontinental Air Transport (TAT), the Lindbergh Line.

TAT was financially stronger than Western Air Express, and more importantly it was better connected politically. After a futile attempt to resist, Hanshue gave in. Western Air Express had to give up to the merged company its Los Angeles–Kansas City route and the related assets. The new entity was named Transcontinental and Western Airlines, or

A Western Fokker goes one better than the cabin radios that were commonly installed in the airlines of the day to entertain passengers. Unless the Fokker landed close to a television transmitter and the passengers carefully set the antenna to watch TV while rescue arrived it is doubtful that the set got much use.

TWA. Hanshue was made president but was a figurehead and left after eight months to pick up the pieces of Western Air Express.

When the dust settled, financially strapped WAE was practically back where it started. It had given up or sold all of its network, except its original Los Angeles–Salt Lake City air mail route with the spur to San Diego, and the truncated routes of its subsidiary, Mid-Continent Air Express. This state of affairs attracted a new owner looking for a bargain. The company that acquired majority control was General Aviation (Manufacturing) Corporation, a subsidiary of General Motors. GM also controlled TWA and Eastern Air Transport, having indirectly assumed the interests of Clement Keys' group when it encountered financial difficulties.

In 1934, like all the other airlines, struggling WAE was hit hard when the task of flying the air mail was given to the Army for four disastrous months on the basis of bid rigging accusations at Walter Folger Brown's so-called spoils conferences. But when the government came to its senses, WAE regained the San Diego–Los Angeles–Salt Lake City route under a new name, General Airlines. Pop Hanshue, however, was forced to resign. As a participant in the spoils conferences he could no longer work in the aviation industry under the terms of Air Mail Act of 1934. The act also specified that aircraft manufacturers could no longer own airlines, so General Aviation had to divest itself of General Airlines. The airline went on the block, but not before General Airlines acquired four DC-2s when it regained its old mail route. By year-end, when the company was sold, so were the DC-2s, not to the new owner, but to Eastern to help pay off General Aviation.

The new majority owner was William Coulter, a Pennsylvania private investor, who gave back the airline's old identity, renaming it Western Air Express

Corporation. His business strategy centered on developing a close relationship with United Airlines as a feeder line and link to Los Angeles via Salt Lake City. Four ex-United Boeing 247s were acquired and WAE tiptoed toward a merger with United.

In 1937 WAE cautiously began expanding its system once again by acquiring National Parks Airways, which extended its route from Salt Lake City up to Great Falls, Montana. In the same year, it acquired its first DC-3, a DST sleeper version.

Following two years of internal wrangling about whether to merge with United, the proposal was put to the CAB in 1940, which promptly turned it down. The West needed an independent regional airline, WAE was told. The CAB did, however, approve an unusual cooperative arrangement between the two airlines. It allowed them to provide joint through-service between Chicago and Los Angeles via Salt Lake City. One airplane would make the entire trip, but it would be flown by a United crew on the Chicago–Salt Lake City segment and a Western crew

A chorus line did its best to hype Western's F-32s on their formal inauguration, but to no avail. The awkward 32-seat giants were gone within two years.

A rare shot of two generations parked side by side illustrates air transportation's fast-paced development in the 1940s and 1950s. The Western Boeing 707 and DC-6 parked side by side are separated by only 10 years. The DC-6 continued to drone along the airways packed full of coach passengers long after the jet set shelled out the stratospheric fares to ride in style at stunning speed. Note the Constellation taxiing out in the background.

between Salt Lake City and Los Angeles. It was the beginning of the interline agreements that became popular after World War II.

In early 1941 WAE decided to recognize the progress it had made since it almost ceased to exist by renaming itself Western Airlines. Air mail would continue to provide an important subsidy, but the company's primary business was flying passengers in a fleet of 22 Boeing 247s and 3 DC-3s.

Like most of its contemporaries, Western Airlines provided excellent service in World War II and reaped important benefits from the experience. Western's chief responsibility was flying a contract schedule for Air Transport Command from Great Falls, Montana, and Seattle, Washington, into Alaska as far as Nome and the whole Aleutian chain, all the way to Attu. In some of the world's most atrocious weather, Western racked up a perfect safety record and one of the highest aircraft utilization rates in ATC. Its DC-3s averaged 12 hours a day, two hours more than the runner-up.

For Western, the greatest wartime gain was the opportunity to rebuild important sections of the route structure it lost at the spoils conference, a decade before. In 1943 it was allowed to restart service between Los Angeles and San Francisco. Returning to this financially lucrative market was one of the most important steps forward for the tenacious airline.

The following year Western absorbed Inland Air Lines, which flew a milk route from Great Falls to Denver and into South Dakota. Thus, by the end of the war the company once again had an extensive if circuitous presence throughout the Rocky Mountains and Southern California, and was ideally poised for a significant postwar expansion.

Western's first big step after the war came in January 1946, when it put in service its first DC-4 on the Los Angeles–San Francisco route. It was the first true, civilian DC-4, not a converted C-54, and it was an instant hit with passengers used to DC-3 service. By the fall, Western was flying 12 roundtrips on the route and had 4 DC-4s in its fleet with more on the way.

Important route awards gave Western the coveted Los Angeles–Denver nonstop sector in late 1945, and put it back on the Los Angeles–Seattle run via Portland in 1947. Extensions were also granted to Mexico City to the south (which wouldn't be served for another decade) and the oil-rich Canadian towns of Calgary and Edmonton to the north. However, the predicted postwar boom turned out to be a bust and Western found itself overextended. The company had to default on its bank loans and sell spare tires to meet the payroll. Orders placed for

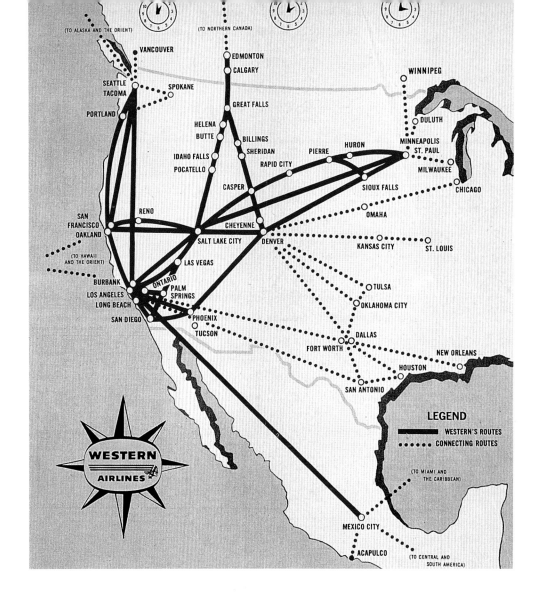

new aircraft, including DC-6s and Convair 240s were in serious jeopardy.

Into this grim situation came a young airline executive, Terrel "Terry" Drinkwater, to take over as president at the behest of the company's creditors. His youthful ambition at a previous job with Continental naively drove him to try and oust its flamboyant president, Robert Six, but he quickly found himself outmaneuvered and out of a job. Western was his chance to run his own show and he would ably guide the airline over the next two decades into the jet age.

Drinkwater needed to raise cash in a hurry and realized that his only real option was to sell one of Western's newly won routes. He reluctantly concluded that the Los Angeles–Denver nonstop route would raise the most cash, and sold it to an eager United for $3.7 million, throwing in four DC-4s. For

This Western route map from the 1950s shows the famous Casper Cutoff (between Salt Lake City and Casper). Prior to obtaining authorization to fly directly to Casper and beyond, Western had to go up north to Great Falls before backtracking. The cutoff opened the Midwest to Western and substantial growth opportunities.

Belatedly Western became a Constellation operator when it acquired Anchorage, Alaska based Pacific Northern Airlines which had six short bodied 749 Connies in its fleet. They were retained by Western for about a year and a half before being sold.

United the route was a big strategic prize, connecting the Mainline's eastern network directly with Southern California. Painful as it was, Drinkwater's strategy saved Western in the nick of time and together with an improving economy set it on a course of steady, sustained growth.

In late 1948 Western had recovered sufficiently to allow it to take delivery of 10 Convair 240s, one of the best equipment decisions it ever made. The 240s were the best airliners available at the time for a short-haul system spanning the Rocky Mountains. Pressurized and powerful, with seating for 40 passengers, they outperformed not only the aging DC-3s but also the unpressurized 44-seat DC-4s. By 1949 Western was again profitable and could concentrate on consolidating its position while preparing for the entry into service of the pressurized DC-6B.

In late 1952 a small but very important route

award rationalized the airline's meandering network north of Salt Lake City and Denver. It was the Casper Cutoff, giving Western direct access to the Midwest from Salt Lake City over Casper, Wyoming, instead of having to fly hundreds of miles north to Great Falls before circling back down. It opened a rational route all the way to Minneapolis, a destination Western was authorized to serve earlier, but couldn't properly exploit. The Twin Cities–Southern California connection turned into one of the company's most profitable long-haul routes in coming years as the increasingly prosperous northerners sought warmth, entertainment, and employment in sunnier climes.

By early 1953 Western was flying five DC-6Bs along the length of the West Coast and to Minneapolis. Additional route approvals came through in the next few years, including service between San Francisco and Denver via Reno, nonstop service between

Denver and Minneapolis, and a Denver–Los Angeles link via Phoenix, Arizona. Service to Mexico City began from Los Angeles as political obstacles were finally overcome a decade after the route was awarded, and the DC-6s also began serving Calgary and Edmonton.

By the mid-1950s, Western served 44 cities in 12 states and 2 countries with a fleet of 33 aircraft and prospered as a regional airline. It had state-of-the-art equipment, but its fleet size limited its strength against the Big Four on competitive routes, so it competed aggressively on quality of service. This era saw the introduction of such Western innovations as Champagne Flights and the famous Hunt Breakfast.

The corks first popped on the Seattle–Los Angeles route and were so successful that extra flights had to be added. For several years Champagne Flight passengers also received a complimentary vial of French perfume to perpetuate their sense of luxury. But while a novelty on U.S. airlines, champagne had flown freely on many foreign carriers from the earliest days, so in a worldly sense Western's move wasn't all that innovative. The Hunt Breakfast, however, was without equal for better or worse.

It was kicked off shortly after the aircraft settled into cruise, with a startling blare of a bugle sounding an alleged hunting charge. Then came the sound of dogs barking and horses thundering through the cabin, followed by a bowler-hatted flight attendant in a red waistcoat. She was pushing a lavish trolley that groaned under the sizzling remains of every farmyard animal imaginable. The FAA soon banished the tape recorder that produced the sound effects, alleging that it might interfere with navigation, but the breakfast remained a hit for years.

By the mid-1950s, Western's most popular spokesman was a sassy yellow TV cartoon mascot called Wally Bird who confidently proclaimed that Western was "the only way to fly" in the company's ad campaigns. And the time was coming when the only way to fly would be by jet.

Western's transition to the jet age began with the selection of the turboprop Lockheed L-188 Electra for first deliveries in late 1959. The Electra fit perfectly the needs of the company's medium-haul routes. But long before it entered service, it set off a bitter 108-day-long pilots' strike. The issue was the third crew member in the cockpit, and it went beyond Western, which was targeted by ALPA as a test case to resolve the issue. Arguing that jet-powered aircraft were more complex to handle, ALPA wanted the third crew member to be a pilot. Western's management dug in its heels and the strike

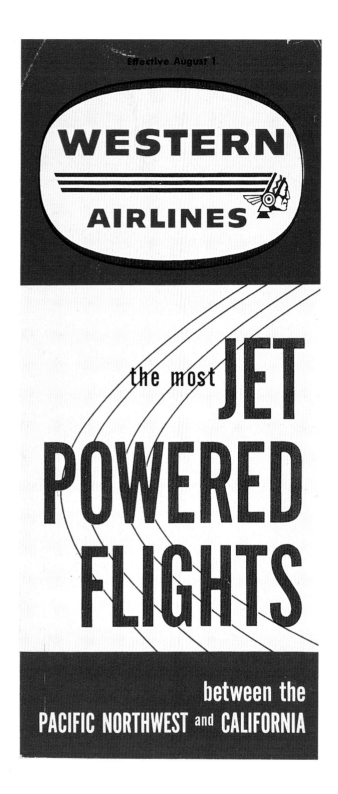

Western was in part motivated to accelerate the introduction of pure jet service because its Lockheed Electras were grounded due to an engine nacelle structural problem. The company had ordered Boeing 720s but successfully scrambled to quickly acquire two Boeing 707s.

On June 1, 1960, Western launched pure jet service with one of two Boeing 707s that were originally intended for Cubana, the Cuban airline. They were embargoed after the revolution and picked up by Western. The airline acquired an additional five 707s in 1968 in anticipation of starting Hawaiian service.

was finally settled by agreeing to table the issue for future resolution.

The Electras were a logical choice, but the long-haul routes presented more of a problem in view of the coming pure jets. They were not sufficiently long to be ideal for the economics of the transcontinental models being developed. It was a problem shared by other airlines and Boeing responded with the Boeing 720B, a lighter derivative of the Boeing 707 with a shorter fuselage. Western initially ordered 4 720Bs and went on to fly 27 of them.

Western's first Electras entered service as scheduled on the Los Angeles–Seattle route, ahead of United's plans to introduce jet service by almost a year. They were well received by the traveling public and put a big dent in United's piston service on the route, when Electra operators suffered a serious setback. Following the Braniff and Northwest Electra crashes caused by an engine nacelle structural defect, the airplane was restricted for nine months to 218 knots in cruise, negating its competitive edge over the piston liners.

Once the Electra was modified, it proved to be a reliable workhorse and Western went on to operate 12 of them for over a decade, replacing the company's piston fleet. But the immediate effect of the Electra crisis drove Western to search for a way to accelerate the introduction of jet service.

Help came from Fidel Castro and the Cuban revolution. Cuba's trade with the United States had been frozen, stranding at the Boeing plant two 707s destined for Cubana, the Cuban national carrier. Western was able to arrange leasing them, launching its first pure jet service on June 1, 1960.

Western later acquired Boeing 720Bs, operating them in large numbers long after most airlines opted for Boeing 727s on the routes they served. Western waited until 1968 to introduce 727 service, and the three-holers shared the skies with the last of the gas-guzzling 720s until 1974.

In the late 1960s, Western achieved several important milestones. In 1967 it expanded into Alaska by buying Pacific Northern Airlines, a line operating a Lockheed Constellation and Boeing 720 fleet connecting Alaska with Seattle and Portland, and still run by the colorful bush pilot who started it in 1932.

The following year Western introduced its first short-haul jet, the Boeing 737, which would become a mainstay of its fleet. Compatibility with the Boeing 720 fleet and better meeting Western's needs than the DC-9 at its high-altitude airports were primary considerations for selecting the 737.

In 1968 important changes also occurred in Western's ownership. The company attracted the

In this curious photo the flight attendant is wielding a Boeing fan-jet brochure but the interior is distinctly un-Boeing. The vortex hairdos, however are a clear sign that the jet age has arrived.

interest of Kirk Kerkorian, a highly successful self-made financier, who had built and sold a substantial supplemental carrier, Trans International Airlines. Looking for another aviation venture, he acquired 27 percent of Western's stock, a move taken badly by Terry Drinkwater, who fought Kerkorian's initiatives to influence running the company and was forced out within two years. Concurrently, mergers were considered with Continental and American Airlines. The latter option won board approval from both parties, but the CAB turned down the proposal, and shortly thereafter Kerkorian reduced his holding in Western.

The year 1969 brought another long-sought route award. After trying for a decade, Western finally won approval to service Hawaii from Los Angeles (and also from Anchorage, given the Alaskan presence it had acquired in the meantime). But the field had become crowded and the Los Angeles award wasn't as lucrative as Western had hoped. Continental, TWA, and Northwest were also approved to compete on the route, and Pan Am and United were already there. All the airlines had 747s on the route except Western.

Western initially served Hawaii with five Boeing 707-347s acquired for the purpose. They experienced good load factors, primarily because its competitors' 747s were experiencing teething problems with engine reliability. And Western's own widebodies weren't long in coming.

American Airlines had taken four options on DC-10s pending the proposed merger with Western, and when it fell through, Western took over the positions. The DC-10s were delivered in 1973 and proved highly successful throughout Western's more densely traveled long-haul routes.

By the time the airline industry was rocked by the oil crisis from which it would not emerge as its former self, Western had become one of its major players even by national standards. Together with good management, its entrenched regional franchise put it in a strong position to weather the upheavals to come. And in 1987 it took its last logical step in the brave new world of deregulation by merging with Delta, the airline that had been the strongest regional and needed Western to become one of the strongest nationals.

Western was an early customer for the Boeing 737. The company selected it over the Douglas DC-9 because it better met Western's needs at its high-altitude airports and had commonality with the other Boeings in the fleet.

Bibliography

Allen, Oliver. *The Airline Builders.* Alexandria, VA: Time-Life Books, 1981.

Arend, Geoffrey. *La Guardia, A Picture History.* New York: Air Cargo News, 1979.

Arend, Geoff. *Newark, A Picture History.* New York: Air Cargo News, 1978.

Bender, Marylin, and Selig Altschul. *The Chosen Instrument.* New York: Simon and Schuster, 1982.

Bernstein, Aaron. *Grounded, Frank Lorenzo and the Destruction of Eastern Airlines.* New York: Simon and Schuster, 1990.

Birtles, Philip. *Lockheed Tristar.* Shepperton, England: Ian Allan, 1999.

Boeing Historical Archives. *Boeing Model 307 Stratocliner.* Seattle.

Boeing Historical Archives. *Boeing Model 377 Stratocruiser.* Seattle.

Borman, Frank, with Robert Serling. *Countdown.* New York: Morrow, 1988.

Brock, Horace. *Flying the Oceans (Memoirs of a Pan American pilot and senior executive).* New York: Aronson, 1978.

Cleary, George Jr. *American Airlines, America's Leading Airline.* Dallas: 1982.

Cleary, George Jr. *Braniff, With a Dash of Color and a Touch of Elegance.* Dallas: 1981.

Cleary, George Jr. *Eastern Airlines, An Illustrated History.* Dallas: 1985.

Cleary, George Jr. *National, Airline of the Stars, A Pictorial History.* Dallas: 1995.

Cohen, Stan. *Wings to the Orient, Pan American Clipper Planes, A Pictorial History.* Missoula, MT: Pictorial Histories Publishing Co., 1985.

Cook, William. *The Road to the 707.* TYC, 1991.

Daley, Robert. *An American Saga, Juan Trippe and His Pan Am Empire.* New York: Random House, 1980.

Davies, R. E. G. *Airlines of the United States Since 1914.* McLean, VA: Paladwr Press, 1998.

Davies, R. E. G. *Delta, An Illustrated History.* McLean, VA: Palawdr Press, 1990.

Davies, R. E. G. *Pan Am, An Airline and its Aircraft, An Illustrated History.* New York: Orion Books, 1987.

Endres, Günther. *McDonnell Douglas DC-10.* Shrewsbury, England: Airlife, 1998.

Forty, Simon. *American Airlines.* Shepperton, England: Ian Allan, 1997.

Forty, Simon. *United Airlines.* Shepperton, England: Ian Allan, 1997.

Gann, Ernest. *Fate is the Hunter.* New York: Simon and Schuster, 1961.

Germain, Scott. *Lockheed Constellation and Super Constellation.* North Branch, MN: Specialty Press, 1998.

Glines, Carroll, and Wendell Moseley. *The DC-3.* Philadelphia: Lippincott, 1966.

Hudson, Kenneth, and Julian Pettifer. *Diamonds in the Sky, A Social History of Air Travel.* London: Bodley Head, 1979.

Jones, Geoff. *Delta Air Lines.* Shepperton, England: Ian Allan, 1998.

Jones, Geoff. *Northwest Airlines.* Shepperton, England: Ian Allan, 1998.

Juptner, Joseph. *U.S. Civil Aircraft Series, Volumes 7, 8, 9.* New York: McGraw Hill, 1994.

Lindbergh, Anne Morrow. *Listen! The Wind.* New York; Harcourt, Brace and Co., 1938.

Lindbergh, Anne Morrow. *North to the Orient.* New York: Harcourt, Brace and Co., 1935.

Mahoney, Lawrence. *The Early Birds, A History of Pan Am's Clipper Ships.* Miami: The Pickering Press, 1987.

Moore, Byron. *The First Five Million Miles.* New York: Doubleday, 1955.

Morgan, Len. *Reflections of a Pilot.* Blue Ridge Summit, PA: TAB, 1987.

Morgan, Len. *View From the Cockpit.* Manhattan, KS: Sunflower University Press, 1985.

Nance, John. *Splash of Colors, The Self Destruction of Braniff International.* New York: Morrow, 1984.

Nebelsick Mahler, Gwendolyn. *American Airlines Flight Attendants, A Pictorial History.* Marceline, MO: Walsworth Publishing Company.

Norris, Guy, and Mark Wagner. *Boeing.* Osceola, WI: MBI Publishing Company, 1998.

Norris, Guy and Mark Wagner. *Douglas Jetliners.* Osceola, WI: MBI Publishing Company, 1999.

Pearcy, Arthur. *Douglas Propliners.* Shrewsbury, England: Airlife, 1995.

Pearcy, Arthur. *Sixty Glorious Years, A Tribute to the Douglas DC-3 Dakota.* Shrewsbury, England: Airlife, 1995.

Reed, Dan. *The American Eagle.* New York:

St. Martin's Press, 1993l

Ruble, Kenneth. *Flight to the Top (a pictorial history of Northwest Airlines).* Viking Press, 1986.

Rummel, Robert. *Howard Hughes and TWA.* Washington, D.C.: Smithsonian, 1991.

Serling, Robert. *Eagle, The Story of American Airlines.* New York: St. Martin's Press, 1985.

Serling, Robert. *From the Captain to the Colonel, An Informal History of Eastern Airlines.* New York: The Dial Press, 1980.

Serling, Robert. *Howard Hughes' Airline, An Informal History of TWA.* New York: St. Martin's/Marek, 1983.

Serling, Robert. *Maverick, The Story of Robert Six and Continental Airlines.* New York: Doubleday, 1974.

Serling, Robert. *The Electra Story.* New York: Doubleday, 1963.

Serling, Robert. *The Jet Age.* McLean, VA: Time-Life Books, 1982.

Serling, Robert. *The Only Way to Fly, The Story of Western Airlines.* New York: Doubleday, 1976.

Serling, Robert. *When the Airlines Went to War.* New York: Kensington, 1997.

Solberg, Carl. *Conquest of the Skies, A History of Commercial Aviation in America.* Boston: Little Brown, 1979.

Steele, Donna. *TWA Cabin Attendants, Wings of Pride, A Pictorial History.* Marceline, MO: Walsworth Publishing, 1985.

Stringfellow, Curtiss, and Peter Bowers. *Lockheed Constellation.* Osceola, WI: MBI Publishing Company, 1992.

Taylor, Frank. *High Horizons (A History of United Airlines).* New York: McGraw-Hill, 1964.

Thomas, Don. *Airline Artistry.* Dunedin, FL, 1992.

Thomas, Don. *Nostalgia Pan Americana.* Dunedin, FL, 1987.

Thomas, Don. *Poster Art of the Airlines.* Dunedin, FL, 1989.

Wall, Robert. *Airliners.* Secaucus, N.J.: Chartwell Books, 1980.

Williams, Brad. *The Anatomy of an Airline (A History of National Airlines).* New York: Doubleday, 1970.

Yenne, Bill. *Northwest Orient.* New York: Gallery Books, 1986.

index